The Untherapist

Surviving Divorce, Remarriage, Tornadoes, Rip Currents, and Other Forces of Nature

By Anne-Lise Jasinski

The Untherapist: Surviving Divorce, Remarriage, Tornadoes, Rip Currents, and Other Forces of Nature

Copyright @ 2020 by Anne-Lise Jasinski

All rights reserved in all media. No part of this book may be used or reproduced without written permission, except in the case of brief questions embodied in critical articles and reviews.

The moral right of Anne-Lise Jasinski as the author of this work has been asserted by her in accordance with the Copyright, Designs, and Patents Act of 1988.

Chapter opening illustrations © 2020 Kayla Hollis

Author photograph by Chasing Amber Photography

Published in the United States by BCG Publishing, 2020.

http://www.BCGPublishing.com

Dedication

For Tom, obviously. ;-)

Disclaimer

The author has tried to recreate events, locales and conversations from her most accurate memories of them. Some names and identifying details have been changed to protect the privacy of individuals from whom consent was unable to be obtained.

Anne-Lise: The Untherapist is not a professionally licensed organization. Anne-Lise Jasinski is not a psychologist, psychiatrist, or professionally licensed therapist and has no formal medical training from any organization. All content provided within this book is for personal use and is not intended to diagnose, treat, prescribe, or cure any illness or disease, whether physical, emotional, mental, or of any other nature.

No content should be construed as a prescription, promise, cure, or advice of any kind. Any information, instruction, or suggestion offered is not medical advice or a substitute for professional medical and psychological diagnosis and care. Do not discontinue or modify any medication presently being taken without proper medical advice from your professional health care provider.

Anne-Lise: The Untherapist is not responsible for any adverse effects. Use of this book and its accompanying resources constitutes your agreement to having read and understood this information and indicates that you assume complete responsibility for your own well-being on all levels at all times.

The author is not affiliated with any religious organization. She uses the word "Divine" to indicate the existence of an entity referred to in various cultures and belief systems as Higher Power, God, The Universe, Source, Allah, Buddha, and Great Spirit, among many others. Untherapy does not assume or require adherence to any specific spiritual practice. Untherapy is useful for any person who desires a deeper understanding of human behavior and connection.

Table of Contents

Introduction

What this book is: I wrote this book for you, my new friend. We haven't been formally introduced (yet), but I promise: by the end of this book, you are going to know me better than you know some of your closest friends and relatives. Over the past ten years of becoming the Untherapist, I have discovered that everything is understandable. In writing this story down, I haven't held back anything about that messy process. I want you to see how it all works together, the bad and the good, the hard and the easy, so you can begin to believe that the same is also possible for you.

Looking back, if I could've had one thing to help me get from the Chapter 1 version of myself (stuck, codependent, triggered, miserable, powerless) to the Chapter 12 version of myself (spoiler alert: I end up happy, healthy, empowered, and super in love with my life and my people), I would've wanted someone to simplify the struggle and show me what to do about it. Not in a controlling kind of way, but in a way that returned me to my own inherent ability to heal and learn. I would've wanted someone to reach into the darkness of my fears and turn on the light so I could see what the hell was going on. I would've wanted someone to explain in plain language (that even my overwrought mind could understand) why the people I loved were all acting crazy. And why, no matter how hard I tried, I couldn't seem to feel better, improve my circumstances, or like the person I saw in the mirror.

What this book is not: This book is not a magic bullet. It will be for you exactly what you want and need it to be. Do the work, and you will get results. I do not claim to be a medical doctor, mental health professional, or certified anything.

How this book is organized:

1) The book is divided into two parts: Chapters 1-8 are "The Making", in which my life is about forcing things to happen the way I think they are supposed to. Part Two (Chapters 9-12) is "The Becoming", in which I gradually learn to trust that the divine trajectory of my life is ever improving and eventually stop trying to manage all the "things."

2) At the beginning of each chapter is a section called "Chapter Framework". This is included to give you a lens through which to view the stories that follow. Every chapter framework includes two perspectives:

    a) <u>Old Belief (without Untherapy)</u>: This is what I believed at the time this chapter was happening. It is the set of rules that informed my life view and explained my choices. As counterproductive as many of those choices were, knowing the context will help illustrate how I created the end results I then grappled with. Keep in mind that at the time, I was not self-aware enough to even recognize that I had these beliefs. I simply acted out my subconscious programming in the way that felt most safe and right for me.

    b) <u>The Untherapist Perspective</u>: This section illuminates the understandings I now have as I look back on this portion of my life story and realize what was happening on a deeper level. Keep in mind, until I started practicing Untherapy as a lifestyle, these lessons were not part of my awareness in the moment that these stories were happening. They encapsulate the wisdom I have gathered through doing this work over time.

3) At the end of the book, I've included an Appendix as an additional reference. Here, I detail the components of the Untherapy Model of Human Behavior and illustrate the ways they interact with one another

to form your cohesive self. I also include the core perspectives of the Untherapy system in their current (and ever-evolving) form.

How to use this book:

1) Entertainment: This book contains the pertinent details of my life as they influenced the development of Untherapy. My journey to becoming Anne-Lise: The Untherapist includes a lot of juicy stories that read like a riveting work of fiction. They would be an entertaining way to pass a Sunday afternoon. If that's what you need right now, bounce lightly over the lesson frameworks at the beginning of each chapter and don't bother downloading the bonus study guides mentioned at the end of each chapter.

2) Education: If you're into personal development and love educating yourself on the different personality theories that are out in the world, pay special attention to the lesson frameworks at the beginning of each chapter. You may also benefit from the Appendix at the end of the book, where you will find an overview of the Untherapy Model of Human Behavior.

3) Transformation: If you are looking for a deeper understanding of yourself and others, or if you're into maximizing your relationships and discovering new ways to assume personal responsibility for all the ways you are creating your reality right now, make sure you take advantage of the bonus downloadable resources mentioned at the end of each chapter. Work through the ones that really light you up and watch how these concepts illuminate the dark corners of your mind. Untherapy is holistic, addressing thoughts, emotions, and behaviors from many angles. The approach is gentle and gradual. If you make an

intentional practice of these principles, over time you will notice major changes. There is also the occasional spontaneous evolution, where your healing seems to culminate in a sudden "whoosh" of growth that happens all at once. Regardless of pace, it is all working in your favor with perfect timing.

What you can do next (if you like this book):

1) Leave a good review! Help other people find this book more easily by letting them know why you enjoyed it and how it helped you.

2) Share it with your friends! Loan your copy out, or even better, buy a few extra copies and give them as gifts.

3) Join the Untherapy Academy! Go to theuntherapist.com/UntherapyAcademy to learn more about making Untherapy part of your own lifestyle. The Academy offers:

    a) Ongoing weekly live interactive support

    b) Access to an ever-expanding library of essential on-demand courses

    c) Membership in a distraction-free community of like-minded people

    d) Additional bonuses and resources to help you simplify and enjoy your relationships

PART ONE

The Making

Chapter 1

How Did You Get So Messed Up?

Chapter Framework:

Old belief (before Untherapy): Life happens to me. Despite my best efforts to be good, I end up in hard places that feel unfamiliar and out of alignment with who I am. Stress and fear are my perpetual companions, so familiar that I don't even notice their omnipresence. I feel out of control and need to be rescued.

The Untherapy Perspective: Rock-bottom moments are gifts that call us to divine relief and healing. When we see ourselves through someone else's eyes and realize we don't relate to our own image, that cognitive dissonance sets up the optimal platform for change. In this state, we are primed to consider new possibilities for our life. We are much more likely to take a new course of action and believe that something could change. Therefore, it does.

"A journey of a thousand miles begins with a single step." –Lao Tzu

"You want me to shut the door?" I reach to close it behind me as I step into the attorney's luxurious office.

He looks up from his cherrywood desk and gives me a slow, lecherous scan from stem to stern. I pause, mid-stride, awaiting his cue. "Better leave it open," he instructs.

My face flushes—I've been made. I was going for "subtle sexy that inspires a discount", not "will barter for services rendered". I may have overplayed my hand here. I glance out at his paralegal to see if she heard. Her deadpan expression tells me she knows the drill. I glance down at my fitted sundress and instinctively clasp my arms over my chest like it's a little chilly. Then I shift my gaze past his coiffed hair and expensive suit at the downtown bustle shimmering thirty stories below us in the Texas heat.

I take a quick breath for courage and arrange myself in the gorgeous red leather armchair directly across from him. "You're okay," I whisper deep in my heart. "The only way out is through." This phrase has given me courage to do so many hard things ever since my midwife Susie introduced it during my first home birth. I think of my firstborn Gideon now. I remind myself why I'm even here in this overpriced office, my thirteenth attempt to find the right lawyer.

"My son has been kidnapped, and I need you to get him back for me," I begin, my voice bolder than I intended.

As Mr. Lecherous jots down notes, I weave the tale of my woes: married to an abusive husband who recently ran off with another woman. While my kids were spending the last week of summer with their dad, without my knowledge or permission he unenrolled my two oldest (ages eight and ten) from the only school they've ever known and put them in the one closest to his new home, thirty miles away. He returned the two youngest (ages four and six) because it just "made more sense." In other words, they are more work, so Mom should do it (obviously). He has since returned my eight-year-old daughter (apparently, she proved to be too much work also), but he insists that Gideon should stay with him permanently.

I measure my words deliberately, taking care to avoid the tender knife pricks in my soul that haunt me every moment since my son was taken. I secretly fear I don't even deserve to be able to raise these kids, but I don't let myself think that now. I have to be "on". I must sell this so he will help me. Mr. Lech asks why I've waited almost a year to seek legal counsel. I feign confidence and explain the parenting plan we amicably agreed upon when he first left me ten months ago. He asks more about the abuse: when did it start, where did he hit me, did he ever hit the kids, did I ever report it?

My narrative is concise and clinical, just like I rehearsed:

"We've been married eleven years. He started beating me five years ago. He always hit me where no one could see the bruises, mostly abdomen and head (where my hair covers). I was a committed and supportive wife, so it never seemed right to report it. He never hurt the children, but I'm convinced that is because I was always watching. I don't know what he's capable of doing to my son now that I'm not there to protect him."

As I wrap up the pertinent details, Mr. Lech leans back in his chair and clasps his hands thoughtfully behind his head. I steady my gaze to meet his. "You're obviously a smart woman, and beautiful…" He lets his eyes fondle my body again for a moment before continuing. "How did you get here?" The question catches me off guard. In an instant, I am transported back to a childhood memory.

Voices outside the tent rouse me awake. It's a chilly summer morning in The Boundary Waters Canoe Area Wilderness of Minnesota. My sister Stephanie is still sound asleep next to me. I stretch luxuriously, enjoying the warmth of my goose down sleeping bag while remembering how hot I would be waking up back home in Texas right now. Natural air conditioning, my dad calls this northern climate.

As my groggy mind clears, I identify the voices as belonging to my dad and my younger brother Jonathan. My older brother Neil is already at college, so he didn't come along for this trip. They're saying something about bears? I put my shoes on and step out of the tent to see that they are investigating giant paw prints all around our tents. Dad explains that this is why it's so important to string our food up in the trees like we do. He reminds us of the importance of selecting the right size of tree limbs that are strong enough to hold the food bags but too fragile for the bears to climb out on. He also makes a point to reiterate that we should never eat in our tents, because the bears will smell the food and want to come in. And that is that.

Mom cooks up the fish Jonathan caught this morning, and we enjoy some freshly picked blueberries my younger sisters, Abigail and Ruth, found nearby. I add a few pieces of dried yogurt from my backpack. It's my favorite, so I've bartered most of my beef jerky for my siblings' shares of dried yogurt to be able to have some at every meal. We break camp and load up for another full day of gorgeous views, untouched wild country, canoeing and portaging. It will be six more days before we see another human.

And that was how it was growing up. We took these adventures every single summer, backpacking and canoeing through the wilderness. We ate food Mom had prepared from scratch for weeks prior to the trip, drinking water straight out of streams and lakes as we went. I didn't worry about bears or giardia or anything. Dad would protect us, and Mom would make sure we were never hungry.

When we weren't on our annual "summer trip", as we called it, we lived pioneer-style, way past the outskirts of town. The various modest farmhouses I grew up in always had a small boys' room (occupancy two), a small girls' room (occupancy four), and a third (even tinier) bedroom for my parents. We always had only one bathroom, no air conditioning, and no TV. We girls were required to wear dresses to school. We raised our own food, with a large flock of chickens, a milk cow, and a massive garden of over an acre within which each child was required to plant and care for their own crops. I planted a lot of zinnias because they were hardy and required very little care.

My parents were avidly health conscious. We were not allowed to eat sugar, white flour, or other refined and processed foods. Mom and Dad had every home remedy imaginable to cure any sickness. In fact, I never once went to the doctor during my entire childhood. Dad even acted as midwife to deliver the last four of their children. When, as an adult, I decided to hire a midwife to attend my own home births, I felt so over the top.

Dad was the head of the house. Mom submitted and supported him. We kids were obedient and knew the business end of Big Brown, the paddle that delivered justice and kept us all in line. My parents never raised their voices at us or each other. We simply did what we were told, and that was that. My life was orderly, predictable, and safe. I knew the rules. I knew how to stay out of trouble. I knew what I could secretly get away with if I really wanted to. I was in control. It made sense.

Mr. Lech clears his throat and taps his pen impatiently on the shiny desktop, jolting me back to the present. "How did I get here?" I hastily repeat. I collect my thoughts for another moment. How *did* I get here? I'm hussied up trying to garner some sympathy from a greasy high-powered divorce attorney who would take my body without hesitation if he knew he could get away with it. I know how to get the kind of attention needed to get a job done. I've been practicing that for years now. I'm also used up, desperate, and terrified that my son is gone forever.

"It didn't happen all at once," I venture hesitantly, no trace of my thin veneer of self-confidence. Suddenly, I must justify my decisions so this lawyer will believe that I'm worth his time. I don't know how to do that. This guy will obviously not be the one to help me. I conclude with a weak attempt: "It's not like it happened all at once. I guess it was really just one tiny step at a time."

And now, my dear reader, I invite you along on my journey of a thousand steps, so that you may understand how I got here.

****

If this chapter finds you at rock-bottom, and you're ready to turn your difficult situation into an opportunity for redemption, please go to theuntherapist.com/chapter1 and download the study guide. Your timing is perfect, and your healing is ready to happen.

Chapter 2

Moms Don't Get to Have Their Own Lives

Chapter Framework:

-Old belief (before Untherapy): I am a product of my upbringing. I must rebel against those things I did not like about my childhood in order to avoid them. Despite my best efforts, it is likely I will still end up accidentally becoming my mother, and not in a good way. Because I was born a woman, I am doomed to a life of servitude to the patriarchy.

-The Untherapy Perspective: We learn our foundational ideas about feminine nature from the influences of our childhood primary caregivers. Every person carries a mixture of both "Being" (feminine) energy and "Doing" (masculine) energy. Therefore, our core feminine programming can come from both women and men and may include anyone who had a significant impact on us, not just parental figures. Our understanding of such "Being" energy qualities as creation, intuition, community, sensuality, and collaboration become solidified by the time we are about five years of age. As children, our brains naturally accept this specific core programming as normal. Unless we learn how to change it, we unconsciously perpetuate and reinforce this unique programming, for better or worse, for the rest of our lives. Once we become aware that we can change this programming, however, we are free to remove any obstacles to creating our deepest desires.

"She was powerful not because she wasn't scared but because she went on so strongly, despite the fear." –Atticus

"Want to come drink some wine with me?" My mom is pouring two generous glasses of her delicious homemade blackberry wine as if she already knows my answer.

I'm caught off guard for a moment. Wine and beer are a normal part of our household, and we kids always get a sip when we ask for it, but a glass that size? Dad is in Russia on a business trip, and the rest of my siblings are already in bed. In all my sixteen years, she has *never* asked me to drink wine with her. I glance around. "Me?" I ask for clarification.

She leans in with a knowing look. "I found your diary and I have some questions. Let's talk."

My mind seizes with terror as my heart sinks with a thud. I'm toast. Dad grounded me for two months when he found out I was bumming Little Debbie snacks off my friends at school. Pretty sure I'm destined for the firing squad on this one. I'm scrambling in vain to remember what exactly I even wrote in that stupid diary. It definitely involves my recent party escapades…with boys, on the weekends when I visit my brother at college. How am I going to get out of this one?

Mom puts a gentle arm around my shoulder. "You're not in trouble. C'mon." She grabs the wine.

She lights a candle on the dresser, and we arrange ourselves cross-legged on her bed like a couple of best friends at a sleepover. I'm torn between "This is so cool!" and "I'm definitely dead." I take a deep breath and decide to be as honest as I can. At least Dad is on the other side of the world at the moment. It makes the promise of impending doom a bit more manageable, at least for now.

She takes a big sip of wine and begins. "What did you mean when you wrote that you 'love sleeping with guys?'"

"Oh, that?" I laugh with nervous relief. "Maybe it's not your first preference for your daughter, but I feel solid about it. Do you even know what my friends are doing?" I assume she does not know, since I have never had a conversation about sex with either of my parents. I saw them hold hands walking into church one time, and my sister and I almost died of embarrassment. I have never seen them kiss.

I explain that I just enjoy the closeness of cuddling. It's nice and makes me feel less alone. Mom lets out an audible sigh of relief. It bothers me that she doesn't know me better. Has she not noticed how much I care about being a good girl? I explain my make-out protocol. When I meet a new guy I like, I have "the talk" with him. I start by explaining that I'm a virgin and that will not be changing tonight or any time before I get married. I clearly define the rules and boundaries and inform him that if he doesn't push past any of those, we can cuddle and sleep together for the rest of the night. Works like a charm every time!

I reassure Mom that no guy has ever tried to push the limits. I do not elaborate on the exact physical boundaries that I currently enforce. I do not go into detail about the gradual expansion of these boundaries over the past year since my first kiss. I just emphasize the important part. I am a virgin, and that will not change until my wedding night. I'm taking every precaution to ensure that.

Since this is the first time I've ever shared any personal feelings about boys with my mom, we have some catching up to do. We drink our wine and giggle, talking late into the night. She wants to know more about who I have a crush on, which annoys me, because she doesn't seem to comprehend that I don't want to be tied down. I don't have a boyfriend and am not looking. I don't like the idea of being with the same one every time. I've tried it here and there. He always starts to get possessive and controlling. I never make it past two weeks, at which point I unceremoniously dump him like last week's garbage and move on.

I've been referred to as a man-eater more than once. I don't care. I like to be in charge. She wants to know why I feel like that. I don't know how to tell her that I don't want to end up like her—with no freedom and no personal identity. I don't have the heart to admit that I don't respect her. I don't ever see her doing what she really wants. I don't even *know* what she would want, even if she could have it. All she does is take care of her husband and her kids. I will not be caught in that trap. No, thank you!

In the flickering candlelight, Mom's face looks softer and younger. I don't know this side of her. Normally, I would be too uncomfortable to see her this vulnerable, but the wine has softened my hard edges. In this moment, I can imagine her like me, with a head full of dreams and a heart full of hope. She seems so real, so normal, just like a regular person.

I share more details about my ideal "type" and who I hope will ask me to church prom, not as my boyfriend, I remind her, but just as a stand-alone date. I almost feel sad for her. Does she ever get to do this? She doesn't have any girlfriends that I know of. She never goes anywhere by herself to do something just because she wants to. But I don't say any of that. I don't want to risk spoiling the moment for myself.

I flash back to a couple weeks ago when she was fitting me for a new school dress. She has been sewing clothes for me my whole life—100 percent cotton because it's natural and the Old Testament says not to mix fabrics. I love going to the sewing store to select the pattern and fabric with her. I wince with hot shame as I remember the disdain and anger in my voice as I barked orders: "This waistline is gapping! See how fat it makes me look? You're going to have to take in that dart in the back. It makes my butt look way too big. It's puckering! Mom, I told you I wanted a *fitted* skirt."

I recall her cold, determined eyes. She just took my abuse. She didn't even argue with me. Her sewing machine light glowed late into the night as she fixed her mistakes. In the morning, my new dress was hanging beside my bed, perfectly pressed, with a handwritten note from the "ironing fairy" pinned to the shoulder.

As Mom rinses our wine glasses, I head to bed. I can't shake the haunting realization: I'm a bad daughter. I'm mean to my mom, and she doesn't deserve it. I'm going to really try to be more kind to her.

A week later, Dad grounds me for "what I've been doing on the weekends." I'm not allowed to visit my brother anymore. Never mind, I think. Mom betrayed me. I mean, I want her to be happy, but not at my expense. I knew I couldn't trust her. I will never keep a diary again. That way, what I do in secret can't ever be proven. I am in charge. I do what I want. It is not safe to talk about it with anyone, and they wouldn't understand anyway.

****

If this chapter put you in touch with your mommy issues, and you're ready to get clear on next steps toward dealing with them, download the Study Guide at theuntherapist.com/chapter2.

Chapter 3

The Dad Is Always Right

Chapter Framework:

-Old belief (before Untherapy): I am afraid of male authority figures in my life (of which God is one), as they carry the inborn power to judge me. Their judgment determines my worth as a human. The letter of the law is paramount. To get what I want, I can just bend the spirit of the law to meet my needs.

-The Untherapy Perspective: Every person carries a mixture of both "Doing" energy (commonly referred to as masculine) and "Being" energy (commonly referred to as feminine). Contrary to patriarchal ideologies, "Doing" energy is not inherently superior to "Being" energy. Both are essential for thriving. Each individual's proper balance is only discovered by pursuing our deepest desires with faith and courage. Our personal equilibrium is not determined (or limited) by our gender. Our understanding of such "Doing" energy qualities as risk-taking, adventure, survival, and mental reasoning become solidified by the time we are around five years old. At this formative age, our brain waves are in "receive" mode and naturally accept what we experience as normal. If we discover that we are out of alignment with the "Being" and "Doing" energy balance that is right for us, we can release restrictive programming to restore internal harmony.

"The moment God is figured out with nice neat lines and definitions, we are no longer dealing with God." –Rob Bell

Mom and Dad were high school sweethearts. As far as I know, they were each other's first and only love. I never saw them fight or even so much as raise their voices to each other. In a disagreement, Dad always had the final word, per God's orders. Mom always acquiesced, as the submissive weaker vessel. Their relationship seemed straightforward and simple. As a child, I never once worried about them quitting on each other.

I learned to be an exceptionally good liar growing up. There were so many rules, and my dad was consistent and strict. I hated getting spankings, so I went to great lengths to avoid punishment. I don't remember ever offering an honest, uncoerced confession during my entire childhood. By the time I was ten, I could hold a poker face without altering my breathing while looking directly into the most intimidating gaze I knew: my father's piercing blue eyes. I honed this skill for years. It was the primary way I navigated my various personas: good little Christian girl at home, super smart student at school, and party girl on the weekends. And then one day when I was seventeen, I decided to try the truth.

"Dad?" My question rouses him from intense focus. It's late, and the rest of the house is already asleep. He's in the middle of writing his next book, and I know he writes at night to avoid interruptions. Five kids still living at home in a 900-square-foot house means silence is rare. I stay up late for the same reason. Senior-year honors classes come with a heavy homework load, and I get most of it done between 10 p.m. and midnight. I'm on track to graduate at the top of my class with a full academic scholarship to the university of my choice.

His tiny office, just large enough for a desk, is lined on all sides with floor-to-ceiling bookshelves. Hundreds of volumes, neatly organized by topic, fill every available shelf. This library represents all the things Dad cares most about: soils (including his textbooks from grad school and his PhD dissertation), God, health, religion, marriage, nature, pioneer life, farming, child-rearing. I used to love to stare at the rows and marvel at how all the knowledge from all these books could fit in one brain—his brain.

He finishes the line he is writing, pauses for a moment, and then looks up at me. "Yes?" he queries.

In all my seventeen years, I have never felt more weight riding on an individual moment than I do now. I'm three months from graduation, and lately I've been thinking a lot about what it will be like once I move on to college. I've never spent a day alone in my life. I have no idea what it feels like to be by myself. I keep wondering if there is anything I should still learn before I go.

I have decided it is time to try to crack the enigma that is my father. I have never really understood how he thinks. He's always been larger than life. His word is the law of our family—God's Law. I have begun to consider how that will carry over into my life as an independent adult. Will I still be able to follow all his rules without him physically around to enforce them?

I very much want to be a good girl. Every night of my life, for over seventeen years now, he has gathered the family to read the Bible. I know how God expects His chosen people to behave. Although I take some liberties with the interpretation of some of the more inconvenient rules, I maintain a strictly obedient persona. As far as Dad is concerned, I am the model of a godly young lady. I've had a few minor indiscretions recently, but I've paid my debt to the Divine in the form of temporary loss of privileges, and I'm back on the straight and narrow now.

But what about authentic connection? This is the ethereal concept I'm searching for in this moment. I don't have words for it, and I don't even know what it would look like. God has always been a disassociated, far-away concept, full of power, judgment, anger, and punishment. I don't know how to express the feeling that I'm missing something big—something important. I want to find it before I go on to the next chapter of my life. For the past two weeks, I've been planning and rehearsing different versions of the conversation I just initiated. Now is my moment. I have Dad's attention. I force myself to speak.

"I'm scared of you." It wasn't exactly what I had planned on saying, but honestly, it is the most efficient summary of my truth. And now it's out—outside my mind and hanging in the air between us like a dense fog. My heart is pounding so loud in my ears, I'm not sure I'll be able to hear his response. I hold my breath. This is it. My moment of glory, when I throw caution to the wind and do the bravest thing I know how to do. We are maybe (dare I hope?) mere moments from bridging a vast cavern of emotional distance. We will hug and cry tears of relief and joy. He will reassure me that who I am, at my core, is legitimate and even perfect. I have nothing to fear, and he, just like God, loves me no matter what.

He looks at me searchingly, with those piercing blue eyes I know so well. After another pregnant pause, he replies, "That's silly," and promptly returns to his writing.

I know intuitively what this "silly" means. I started noticing around five years old that I had too much energy for my dad's comfort. I was too boisterous and loved people and attention too much. For peace of mind and stress relief, Dad extolled the virtues of meditating in nature, alone. But I felt best when I was in the biggest crowd of people I could find, preferably the center of their attention. The number one reprimand I received as a child was, "Girls, don't be silly!" With four daughters, he was constantly reminding us to contain our exuberant outbursts. We weren't allowed to squeal or scream or giggle uncontrollably. I took this to mean there was something wrong with me. Every time I was happy, these responses just spilled out of my body without warning. As I've grown into my teenage years, I've learned to control my joy and limit my expression of it to times when I am not around my dad. Hearing the word "silly" in the context of this most important conversation instantly quells any hope for connection. My heart sinks with an unceremonious thud.

When I was four, Dad welded a bunch of recycled metal pipes together to make us kids a jungle gym. As a child, it was one of my very favorite places to play. Many times, I would swing too hard and high, lose my grip, and land flat on my back, knocking the wind out of my lungs. The first time it happened, I was sure it was the end. Over time, though, I learned that I was not, in fact, going to die in that moment. Just because I could not breathe when I fell didn't mean I would never breathe again. I learned to wait, relax, and allow my breath to return. It always did.

This moment feels just like that. I swung too hard and too high. My hopeful heart has just fallen from a great height. The impact has stolen the air from my lungs, and I feel like I'm going to die. I stand in the doorway for a few more long moments, waiting for my lungs to work again. There it is. I feel the air begin to return. I suck in a long, slow, silent breath. See, I tell myself, *you did not die. You survived, and now you know*. I shuffle my leaden legs off to bed in surrendered defeat. In this moment, the truth is clear. Who I am is bad. I must try harder to be good. Even when I move away, God is always watching. I must remember not to be silly, not to do what comes naturally for me. It is not safe to be vulnerable with Dad (or God).

****

If this chapter stirred up your daddy issues in a way that compels you to do something about it, I humbly offer the Chapter 3 Study Guide, available at theuntherapist.com/chapter3.

Chapter 4

Willpower Warrior

Chapter Framework:

-Old belief (before Untherapy): The most important way to be good enough is to force myself to abide by the rules no matter what. The greater my sacrifice and the harder I work, the greater my reward. It is absolutely critical to suppress my own desires in favor of others, especially the men in my life (which includes God). I apply willpower to achieve absolute compliance.

-The Untherapy Perspective: We have an inherent need to feel in control of our life circumstances. It feels dangerous to go against the core programming we grew up with, especially if that programming taught us to ignore our own inner desires. If we consistently practice subverting our desires in favor of external rules, especially in the name of fear and/or survival, we have immense ability to convince ourselves that misery is our birthright. Struggle becomes normalized and feels safer than simplicity and ease. Because life is actually designed for our growth, healing, and thriving, we are wired to release the need to struggle and return to a more natural state of flow.

"It is only when a woman surrenders her life to her husband, reveres and worships him, and is willing to serve him, that she becomes really beautiful to him." –Marabel Morgan

It's the beginning of my senior year of high school, and Dad is discussing the new date for the end of the world. I have heard these doomsday predictions throughout my entire childhood. Every few years, he announces the new date for Armageddon. Although it is terrifying to hear how the world is going to explode into death flames, Dad always reminds us not to be afraid. We are part of God's small chosen group that gets to go to a safe place while all the heathens burn for their sins. I decide that if Dad can protect us from bears that tromp around our tents at night, hopefully he knows what he's talking about here, too.

Each of those dates has come and gone with nary an explanation—just a modified prediction pushed into the future. This current one is set to happen at some point in the year 1992. We can't be exactly sure, because the Bible says no one is allowed to know the day or the hour. Wait, what? That's only a few months away, and 1992 is my year of freedom! Right after graduation in May, I'm moving away to college. Will I still be protected? And more importantly, AM I GOING TO DIE BEFORE I GET TO HAVE SEX?

Thankfully, and despite battling rampant fear and anxiety for the rest of the year, 1992 passes successfully into 1993. Whew! Dodged that bullet! From this point forward, I vow to avoid asking my dad for the updated schedule of global annihilation.

College is an eye-opener. I share an apartment with a shy roommate who is rarely home. For the first time in my life, I experience being physically alone in a space. I get asked on a lot of dates, and I'm surprised to learn that "my dad doesn't allow me to" has lost its power. I fumble for ways to say no without offending, which always comes out sounding like "yes." One of these dates ends with the guy cross-legged on my couch, my head in his lap. He insists on giving me a scalp massage that will "blow my mind", so I lie stiff as a board while the odor of his stinky feet curls my nostril hairs.

Although the massage does nothing for my body, the whole experience certainly impresses upon me the value of employing a simple but firm "no thank you" when I'm not attracted to someone. I still date around and indulge in plenty of make-out sessions followed by all-night cuddling. It feels good to come into my power and make my own life choices. I know I'm banking on the letter of the law, but as long as I do not have intercourse, I am a virgin. I am in good standing with God. I'm proud of myself for making the transition to self-monitoring adult with relative ease. I continue to be an excellent student, maintaining all my scholarships and a 4.0 GPA in my elite honors program. I have no clear career path, but I figure, worst case, I'm setting myself up for success at the graduate level.

By now, it's Christmas break of my freshman year at UT Austin. I am faithfully attending the local Austin congregation of the same church I grew up in. I am still not looking for a serious relationship, but when an eligible bachelor starts attending, I say yes to a date. Brad has just moved to town from out of state and was also raised in this religion. He's six feet tall, with curly black hair, bright blue eyes, and a weak chin. He's four years older than me and installs HVAC systems for a living.

Brad strikes me as average in all ways, but he's sweet, interesting, and attentive. I say yes to another date. We go over my sexual boundary protocol, which has maintained its integrity, unchallenged, through my first nine months as an independent woman. I kiss him. It isn't terrible. By the third date, he's pushing my limits. I reiterate my boundaries. I am a virgin. That will not be changing tonight or any time before I get married.

There is a subtle pressure every time I'm around him. I can't put my finger on it. It feels like I somehow owe him something that I don't quite know how to give. I've never felt this pressure from any of the casual dates I've had over the years. I don't know how to define it, so I chalk it up to the fact that he's my first official boyfriend. Or maybe it has something to do with God's plan for my life. Since Brad is the first church guy I've dated, there is a developing, unspoken sense that we have a future together. I have always known I would marry a member (to maintain the purity of God's chosen people, we are only allowed to marry other members of the same religion), but I brush off the thought for now. Marriage isn't even on my radar at the moment. I'm in school and career mode right now.

A month in, we have exchanged those three little words-I love you. I've never been in love before, so I have no reason to doubt this is it. Almost a year of living on my own has taught me the value of being honest. Without the fear of punishment from my dad, I have discovered that I like how it feels to be vulnerable with my friends. When I tell lies now, I feel that old familiar depression from my childhood. I make a promise to myself that I will always be honest with Brad, especially when I'm scared. I don't ever want to feel silly for having a hard conversation again.

I gather the courage to ask Brad about the pile of unopened mail on his kitchen counter. Six weeks in, he lets me open it. I have zero financial acumen, so I educate myself, make payment arrangements with all his creditors, and begin repairing his credit. By summer, we've moved his sister and mom into my apartment from out of state. I tell him it's because I want to help them get on their feet. In truth, I want an excuse for him to keep his own apartment. Now his mom is around to keep us honest, and I share a bedroom with his sister. This makes it much easier for me to resist his constant pressure to go all the way.

Fall classes start, and he's complaining that I care more about school than him. I let my grades slip for the first time in my life. I try not to resent him. I want to be a good girlfriend. His sister and I get closer. Delilah is close to my age and a lost soul who battles chronic physical and mental health issues. Acting as her therapist makes me feel better about my own quandary.

One particularly difficult night, Delilah decides I'm safe enough to trust with her darkest secret. She takes a slow breath as I squeeze her hand encouragingly. She forces the words out. "My brother raped me." My hand flinches away like she's a hot stove. Just like my childhood jungle gym, I've swung too hard and too high. My heart falls flat on its back with a bone-chilling thud. I wait for my breath to return while my thoughts race ahead. Could she mean a different brother? How old was he when this happened? Can she get him thrown in jail? My childhood did not include anything sexual, not even handholding, and least of all incest or molestation. I die a thousand deaths before I catch my breath.

Without revealing why, I call Brad and ask him to come over. It doesn't occur to me to care if Delilah wants to be same room with him right now. I give their mom a quick rundown, and she starts hysterically wailing about being a failure. When Brad arrives, I meet him at the door with a cold question: "Did you rape your sister?" All three begin screaming and crying, blaming, demanding, justifying. I witness the scene in slow motion, their voices echoing through my brain as I dissolve into the background.

Suddenly, for the first time in my life, I get the urge to run. Without thinking, I bolt for the front door. This is before cell phones, and I don't have a car, so I duck into the stairway of the next apartment building and knock on a neighbor's door. I borrow her phone to call one of my professors. We coordinated a study group last semester, and he's the first person who pops into my head who would be willing to put me up for the night without asking too many questions. I just need a little space to figure out my next step. I hide out in the neighbor's apartment until my professor gets there.

As luck would have it, as he arrives to pick me up, my professor crosses paths with Brad, who is searching the complex to locate me. The professor says it's none of his business, but if that's the guy I'm running away from, maybe I should reconsider. "He seems like a good guy. He was desperate to find you, and he seemed really upset at the thought of losing you."

I take this as a sign from God that Brad really does need me, and I am meant to help him. He's my project, and I can't turn my back on him now. I thank my professor for his kindness. Then I turn around and walk back into Brad's life.

I double down on my commitment to this relationship. I keep supportive scripture references in the forefront of my mind. Love covers a multitude of sins. All have sinned and fallen short of the glory of God. He who is without sin, cast the first stone. I move to a new apartment with a roommate from the university so I can escape Brad's family and put the past behind us. I still have my five-year plan: complete my degree, establish my career, *then* consider settling down. In. That. Order. He's more ready than ever for marriage. I'm less ready.

I take him home to meet my parents, and I'm even brave enough to hold his hand in front of my dad. Dad reprimands me later. If he only knew how hard I'm working to maintain purity, maybe he would be proud of me instead. He also says he doesn't think Brad is a good match for me. That makes me want to prove him wrong. I've already invested so much in this relationship. I imagine that for once, God is on my side rather than Dad's.

I avoid drinking alcohol around Brad. I send him home every night, since even cuddling on the couch with my roommate nearby leads to close calls. This mounting pressure drives me to research. I need relief—some supportive guidance or maybe a mentor. Nobody has answers for a good little Christian girl who is trapped in a perfectly acceptable relationship with the right guy and doesn't know how to get him to hold out. I find a book called *The Total Woman* by Marabel Morgan, which promises to teach me all about being a godly wife. I consume the pages with gusto, eager to discover answers.

This book becomes my new bible. Within its pages I find the secret manual for the perfect Christian woman's life. This must be the same book my mother read so many years ago! I feel like I'm peeking through a private window into Mom's unrevealed life. Each chapter discloses new behind-the-scenes wisdom that surely accounts for her unwavering gracious support and compliance all these years.

Mrs. Morgan promises that all I must do is give my husband my undivided, unconditional support and attention, and all my deepest longings will be fully satisfied for the rest of my life. Then I get to the bottom of page 123. "Your husband wants you to want him sexually. He wants you to enjoy lovemaking as much as he does. If you fail in this area, he is devastated. Down inside, he feels he is an **utter failure**. Believe in him and tell him so. Let him know he's your **special project in life**." (Emphasis added.)

The heavens part. The angels burst into chorus. That's it! Brad's unrelenting pressure is the sole result of me not giving him sex! Oh, how it all makes so much sense now! I already know he's my special project in life. I've patched up his credit. I've played therapist to his mom and sister. I've helped him overcome childhood trauma. I bolster his ego on the daily, rearranging my priorities to fit in and around his so he always feels important and special. The reason none of this is helping him feel better is because I refuse to have sex with him! Now that the light has been switched on, my path forward is clear. As I complete the final pages of *The Total Woman*, a singular purpose resounds in my heart. I want to be a "Total Woman." I need to marry Brad as soon as possible.

Like a perfect old-fashioned gentleman, Brad invites my dad to dinner. Over steak and mashed potatoes, he asks Dad for my hand in marriage. We've decided to throw together a quick wedding over the winter semester break, so it doesn't interfere with my classes. Dad is very concerned about the rush. It never occurs to me that he might be worried about pregnancy. I'm just interested in getting this show on the road, sooner rather than later. The sooner intercourse can commence, the sooner my pressure can be lifted, and I can have my "happily ever after" with the one God has chosen for me. Dad does not voice his actual concern. I do not voice mine. Dad gives his blessing, and we set the date.

The simple afternoon ceremony passes in a blur. I remember to pause for dramatic effect and speak the "or poorer" and "in sickness" at a noticeably louder volume than the other vows "before God and these witnesses." I am reassuring my almost-husband that no matter what we go through, no matter how hard it gets, we are going to be just fine. We are about to have officially sanctioned, God-ordained, legal, marital sex. I remember Marabel Morgan's promise. I am nineteen years old and about to become a "Total Woman."

I gaze into Brad's eyes as we say I do. *My dear, sweet love,* I think to myself, *sex is guaranteed to fix your every problem. No more fear, anger, or depression for you! All the while, the act of giving you my body freely, eagerly, and unconditionally will magically reward me with heavenly bliss and unending desire for more.* I shiver in anticipation.

Just outside of town, we check into the little hotel that will host the most important night of my life. I rush into the tiny bathroom and hastily change into the blue lace negligee I received as a wedding shower gift. The material is scratchy, and the fasteners at the crotch require an advanced yoga pose to navigate. My shaky fingers manage two of the three snaps, and I finally abandon the undertaking for the sake of time and ease of access. I stand up straight, drawing in a deep breath to calm my nerves. I meet my gaze in the little bathroom mirror. Despite the unflattering hue of the fluorescent light flickering overhead, my wedding makeup compliments a face full of anticipation. With a coy smile, I whisper to my reflection, "Now go out there and become a Total Woman!"

Brad is already lying in bed, the covers pulled halfway over his naked body. We have been naked together before, but it has been several months. Too many close calls, so I established a "must remain clothed while making out" rule to keep us honest. Traversing the ten feet from the bathroom to the bed, it occurs to me that I'm bridging the chasm between "what I must not ever let myself think about doing" and "what I must now always want to do." The span is not wide enough to complete the transition. The clock on the bedside table reads 9:38 p.m. as I slip into my side and pull the covers up to my neck. I feel chilly and stiff. I've been looking forward to the moment that is about to happen for as long as I can remember. What is wrong with me? He seems nervous, too.

"You ready?" I smile with mock confidence. He nods meaningfully and climbs on top of me. I fumble with the snaps and open my legs, breathing deeply and willing my body to relax. He finds his way in with relative ease. I wait for some sort of distinct sensation of my hymen breaking, but nothing registers. It's over before I can settle in.

I grab a towel from the bathroom and wipe up. As I climb back in bed, the clock reads 9:47 p.m. I lie still for a few moments, letting the magnitude of the moment wash over me. I am no longer a virgin. I am a woman now. I am Brad's wife. It is official. There is no going back. My thoughts race as I search for my new foundational truths. So many rules and boundaries no longer needed. So much resistance, care, and vigilance can be relegated to the past. I don't have to be a good girl anymore. I breathe a sigh of relief. This will be easier.

Brad turns to me with a broad smile and a wink. His confidence seems to be building. "Ready for round two?" He lasts longer the second time, and after that he wants to try different positions. After round three, I tell him I'm getting sore and tired. He ignores my suggestion for a break, eagerly asking for more. I listen for inner guidance. I hear Marabel Morgan's words: "Your husband wants you to want him sexually. He wants you to enjoy lovemaking as much as he does. If you fail in this area, he is devastated." We go again. And again. With a grateful hug, he finally rolls over and falls asleep. His gentle snores belie the gravity of this experience. My awareness floats up to the ceiling, and from this vantage point, I watch him peacefully sleeping next to my worn-out body. Is this what it feels like to be a Total Woman? Have I succeeded? I shift my legs gently, wincing at the burning sensation of my freshly torn flesh.

What is my life now? Is this it? As I methodically review the familiar pages of Marabel Morgan's book in my mind, a realization creeps over me: she assumed I would enjoy the sex. There was no chapter included about what to do if I didn't. There must be something wrong with me. Or maybe I misunderstood my role. Maybe my pleasure was never the point. Never mind—it's too late now. This is what I signed up for. Brad is my special project in life, and I have just taken the ultimate blood oath to devote my life to assuring his success and happiness.

****

If this chapter stirred up some deep issues around willpowering your way into heaven or otherwise forcing yourself to be good enough to be accepted, while I have you here, may I suggest digging a little deeper? The Study Guide for Chapter 4 is all about it. You can download it at theuntherapist.com/chapter4.

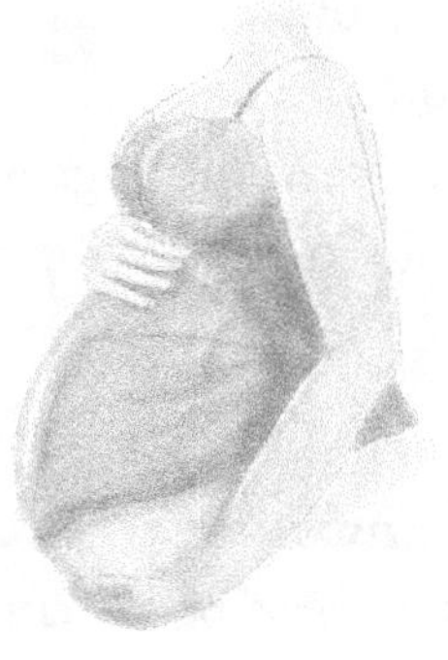

Chapter 5
Victim Vibes

Chapter Framework:

-Old belief (before Untherapy): My ability to enjoy life is not important. My value comes from my performance as a wife and a mother. As a woman, I am not competent enough to be allowed to have an opinion on important issues like my own body, sexual pleasure, loyalty, or parenthood. I exist to meet the needs of others, and if that comes at my expense, at least I get bonus points for martyrdom.

-The Untherapy Perspective: Because life is naturally optimized for our ideal growth, thriving, and happiness, to actively resist this flow is to swim upstream. The tremendous amount of energy it takes to reinforce false beliefs, ignore our intuition, and choose harmful options leaves us feeling exhausted, depressed, invisible, and angry at outside influences. There is nothing sacred about using the Bible to manipulate and control people (even ourselves). Giving up our power of choice is, in fact, also a choice. If we tolerate bad behavior long enough, we might even convince ourselves that it's not, in fact, all that bad. Negative feelings like fear, doubt, and anger are just as useful as positive ones. They draw attention to areas that need healing. As we process and release these emotions, we create space for our own development while also giving others permission to do the same.

"Wives, submit to your own husbands, as to the Lord. For the husband is head of the wife, as also Christ is head of the church; and He is the Savior of the body." –Ephesians 5: 22-23 (NKJV)

As I settle into married life, I habituate to the feeling of disappointment. I teach myself to gauge my success according to Brad's happiness. I decide to consider my lack of sex drive as a blessing. It makes sense to me logically that maybe a woman shouldn't get too carried away with the lusts of the flesh anyway. That seems to be a characteristic more befitting the male gender. The rules are pretty straightforward: always be ready, always say yes, always be attentive, focus only on the positive, stroke his ego and his body as often as possible. Convince him he is an excellent lover.

As I turn twenty and begin my junior year of college, I take a job as a secretary to help out financially. I also discover I am pregnant. Apparently olive oil breaks down the integrity of latex condoms and is therefore not a recommended lubricant. Who reads the warnings on a condom box? My five-year plan is officially dead. The choice to drop out of school is easy enough. I never did figure out a compelling career path, and it seems to be a moot point now that I'm in family mode.

Brad is oddly nervous about my choice. I reassure him I will never regret it. I know deep in my heart that I am doing the right thing—the godly thing. Why does a woman even need a career? I am baffled as I remember the immature girl I was a year ago, prioritizing my education so highly. Why would a woman want to invest that much time and energy into something that would take her away from her husband and kids? My mom had it right all along.

I meet with my professors to inform them of my decision. They plead with me to reconsider, reminding me of how well I am doing and what a bright future I have ahead of me. I brush away their lack of support. They just don't understand. I return the unused money to the scholarship committees that have been funding my education for going on three years now. I square my shoulders, hire a midwife, and prepare for life as a mother.

Giving birth is a life-changing experience. I go into labor at 11 p.m., with contractions starting just five minutes apart. I remember my personal commitment to be kind to Brad so he doesn't feel left out or attacked. I will *not* be one of those unseemly wives who screams and blames her husband for her labor pains. As I ride the waves of acute labor pain, I do my best to lovingly reassure him that I'm just fine.

My midwife Susie guides me through the birthing experience with skill and ease, as her apprentice provides additional support and care. Mom is here, too. She has even brought her famous homemade date-filled cookies for a special post-labor pick-me-up. How did she do this six times, and how did she trust Dad to be her only assistant? I look around the bed and imagine how it would feel if just Brad were here. It's a scary and lonely thought. Three hours later, Gideon has entered the world as our firstborn son. It takes the rest of the night to get all cleaned up, nursed, and settled in for some rest. I am enjoying one of Mom's amazing cookies when it occurs to me that no one ever did this for her. Just then, Brad's 6:00 a.m. alarm goes off. I pop up to make his lunch for work. "Oh no, young lady," midwife Susie insists. "You won't be going anywhere for a while." The reality of juggling motherhood and wifely duties occurs to me for the first time.

Mom stays for a week to help. She handles everything from washing cloth diapers to making Brad's dinner. I am free to master the art of nursing and take catnaps every time Gideon sleeps. When it is time for Mom to leave, I stand on my apartment balcony and watch her drive away, clutching my new baby tightly to my chest. I am overwhelmed at the enormity of this new task. Can I do this? Can I be the mother this little boy deserves?

Gideon is the new love of my life. I didn't know I could adore another human being so much. Brad has a better job now—selling HVAC products—so with a bit of strict budgeting and coupon clipping, I'm able to be a stay-at-home mom. It is bliss. I finally understand how my mom could give her whole life to this.

Around Gideon's first birthday, Brad starts expressing jealousy over the bond I have with our son. Just like when we were first dating, there is once again an ever-present unspoken pressure. Brad wants more from me, more of me. Only this time, I have nothing more to give. He becomes more pensive, distant, and agitated. I am consumed with being a good wife and mother, and I'm baffled at his mental state. I beg him to open up to me, and he finally accuses me of having an affair. His theory is that a man is coming over during the day while he is at work to have sex with me. His proof is the toilet seat in the guest bathroom. It's always in the up position. I cackle with equal parts disbelief and relief. Poor Brad and his overactive imagination.

"Gideon wears cloth diapers, remember?" I explain how I rinse them in the toilet *with the seat up* to get rid of the solids before putting them in the washing machine. I point at my unkempt hair and the disheveled t-shirt with breastmilk stains that hangs sloppily over my stretch marks and widened hips. "Do you really think I'm spending my day with *another man*?" I am beside myself with incredulity. What have I done to elicit such paranoia? I add two more items to my daily to-do list: 1) periodic calls to his work to reassure him I'm thinking only of him, and 2) give him more sex.

When Gideon is almost two, we decide to have a second child. We both come from large families and don't want Gideon growing up without siblings. I'm secretly convinced this will break Brad out of his depression and resolve the growing pressure I'm feeling to give him more of something I don't have. Maybe a daughter this time. Maybe that will be just the thing to make him happy.

During this second pregnancy, I experience none of the attentive care Brad gave me during the first one. He is restless and uneasy, like there's an itch he can't scratch. After much prodding, he confesses that our sex life is uninspiring, which has caused him to sink into chronic depression. I redouble my efforts in the bedroom, challenging myself to say yes to all his desires with less hesitation and more agreeability. Brad wants me to shave all my pubic hair. After weeks of intense resistance, I cannot find a valid reason to deny his desire, so I decide to take the plunge. Turns out Brad was right. There is no law in the Bible against it, and I am not, in fact, struck down by lightning.

Through consistent, intentional, repeated practice, I overcome my resistance to positions other than missionary. It would've been easier if they had more spiritual names than "doggie" and "reverse cowgirl". Then I'm back to the Bible to find a decree against anal sex. When I come up empty, I call a sex info hotline from the phone book. The kind lady on the other end assures me it is perfectly safe and normal, but I should only do it if I want to. "But I'm married," I explain. I hang up the phone and decide I must force myself to comply. I remember that I am honoring God by honoring my husband. I recall the martyrs of the Bible. This is a small sacrifice, really.

When we wear out our new repertoire, Brad introduces the concept of "swinging." Yet another term I've never heard before; this one means: the practice of engaging in group sex or the swapping of sexual partners within a group, especially on a habitual basis. I don't bother looking this one up in the Bible. Brad has chosen this. Why should I resist him? The idea of sex with someone besides my husband is terrifying. The two paramount rules of my life juxtapose for an epic showdown: 1) I must please God. 2) I must please my husband.

There is only one way to reconcile this quandary. God must be calling me to deeper submission *through* my husband. I blow the dust off the old Nave's Topical Bible that Dad gifted me as a child for more effective Bible study. I conduct an in-depth exploration of the God-ordained role of a wife. My conclusion is to take the Bible literally. My husband is my leader just like Christ leads the church, and *he is the savior of the body*. I certainly need to be saved. Therefore, it follows that I must trust his guidance in exactly the same way that the church is expected to trust the guidance of God.

My decision notwithstanding, the years I have spent cultivating intentional control over my sexual desires are not easily undone. We start spending a lot of time with another couple from church, and Brad tells me they want to have sex with us. Late one night when we are over at their house, he convinces me to have sex with him on the trampoline in their backyard. He keeps reassuring me they are already asleep. The next morning, he informs me it was a setup and they were watching us through their bedroom window the whole time. Once again, I have that feeling of losing my grip and falling from the jungle gym. This time, when I hit the ground, it is God's voice that brings back my breath. "This is what your husband most desires, and it is your job to help him get it." I apologize to Brad for feeling betrayed and pray for the willpower to overcome my resistance. God is with me, after all.

One relentless step at a time, Brad obliterates my boundaries, until I am lying on a bed with another woman's husband on top of me while my husband lies next to me on top of this man's wife. The mental gymnastics I use to calm my aversion are like the ones I've been practicing during sex with Brad for over three years now. I have my timing down pat—what sounds to make, how to move, what to say and when. Of course, this new arrangement requires an extra level of vigilance. Since the entire point is Brad's satisfaction, I always keep one eye on him and reserve my primary attention for his needs and desires. I monitor the other wife's behavior to ensure that she is working hard enough to meet Brad's needs. I also take care to keep her husband sufficiently occupied so he doesn't detract from Brad's connection with his wife. My awareness floats above my body, noticing my physical movements with detached apathy.

At first, we just use couples from church, but with such a small congregation, we run through our options in a few weekends. At this point, we officially leave the religion we were both raised in. I am not concerned about my standing with God. I am more convinced than ever that the power abides in the man, not the organization. Brad is my leader, and God requires my submission to him. As proof of God's approval, I remind myself of the physical blessings He continues to bestow upon us. Brad just got a raise at work. Our firstborn is a happy, well-adjusted toddler. I'm experiencing a healthy pregnancy. We have a robust social life (especially after dark).

I spend a lot of time outside my body. I work hard to ignore the pit of hardening resentment located somewhere deep beneath the growing baby inside me. Sometimes when Brad hugs me, stomach acid sears the back of my throat. I soldier on until I am comfortable having sex with whoever Brad puts in front of me.

Brad expands his search for willing couples to swingers' hotlines and newspaper ads. I perfect my phone sex voice to attract potential takers. But as I enter my last trimester, Brad starts coming home from work later and later. He stops arranging our foursomes and isn't sharing his fantasies with me anymore. Although I welcome the break, I know he's up to something else with someone else. We've already crossed so many lines, I'm not sure if cheating is technically possible at this point. But I do feel betrayed that he's doing this behind my back.

One night he doesn't show up for dinner. I promise myself if he doesn't come home tonight, I will have proof of infidelity. Around midnight, I fall into a fitful sleep on the couch. He shows up at 3:30 in the morning, and I confront him. "You've been with another woman, haven't you?" My heart is pounding in my ears as I take shallow sips of air.

"I will only tell you the truth on one condition," he responds. "You have to promise me you won't ask me to stop." There it is again—the falling sensation.

When my heart hits the ground, I drop my head and gently nod. "I promise," I whisper meekly. He in turn promises never to keep another secret about a sexual fantasy or conquest. The next night, he brings his new girlfriend Cindy home for a threesome. To my surprise, this arrangement is more manageable than the foursomes. Since she's already interested in Brad, I don't have to navigate the jealousy factor. I also don't have to deal with any extra testosterone. She's much gentler and more tender than the men. I feel safe enough to inhabit my own body during the entire sexual experience. It's nice.

A month later, my second home birth is attended by my midwife Susie, her apprentice, my mom, my husband, and Cindy. Our beautiful daughter Hannah is a welcome distraction that I'm confident will buy me a few weeks' break. Just three days after the birth, Brad and Cindy have begun arguing and are on the outs. He starts demanding sex from me just a week postpartum. His appetite is growing. With two little ones to care for, I'm already exhausted all the time, but he has his needs. We fall into a pattern of having sex at least once a day during the week and up to five times a day on the weekends. This frequency continues through the end of our relationship.

As Hannah turns a year old, I become pregnant for the third time. I realize a pattern. Brad's sexual appetite spikes when I'm pregnant. By now, I've gotten good at knowing his type and predicting which husbands will cooperate best. Brad is notorious for inflating the wife's response to his sexual prowess. He always needs to feel like an amazing lover and regularly interprets their behavior to mean they are falling in love with him. He develops an elaborate fantasy about us swinging with a couple and the wife immediately running away from her husband to live with us. I play along to keep him happy, reassuring him it will surely happen next time, but his depressive episodes are becoming unmanageable. He grows increasingly anxious, needy, and impatient.

And then it happens. We hook up with a young couple, and the next day, the girl calls us back. She claims she is being abused by her boyfriend and needs help. Brad interprets this as code for "she fell in love with me and needs an excuse to get out." By the end of the week, I've arranged to move her into our home. Celeste is the girl of Brad's dreams and everything I am not. At twenty-four years old and six months pregnant, I am "the old worn-out shoe" he is comfortable coming home to, as he puts it. She is an eighteen-year-old black-haired, porcelain-skinned goddess with a tiny waist and voluptuous breasts. At barely five feet tall, she fits perfectly under my armpit. Responding to Brad's excitement at this dream come true, I decide to not just move her into our house, but right into my place in our family. I empty my closet, grab my toiletries, and change the bed sheets. She is officially his new woman. The first night, I lie awake on the couch for hours listening to their sex noises. I fall from the great height of the jungle gym over and over, until I'm sure I will never breathe again. I sure as hell hope God is paying attention, because He owes me big.

By the second night, I've made a pallet in the front room to share with my two kids. I explain that I am the "old mommy" and that Celeste is the "new mommy". Gideon and Hannah are used to being ignored and neglected, and they are thrilled to have my undivided attention. Celeste doesn't have a car or a job, so she occupies Brad's attention 100 percent of the time when he's home. My presence is required for a threesome about once a week, but otherwise, I am determined to enjoy a blissful vacation from my wifely duties. I cook and clean for Brad and Celeste, but for the first time in six years, I get a break from sex. I play with my kids and enjoy the simple pleasure of a full night's sleep. My pregnant belly is perfectly happy sleeping on the floor, cuddled up with my littles.

****

If you've ever been caught in a cycle of victimhood where you felt utterly controlled by outside forces and unable to escape, you might benefit from digging a bit deeper on this topic. I'd love for you to check out the Chapter 5 Study Guide for more resources on how to escape this cluster and regain your inherent power. Download it at theuntherapist.com/chapter5.

Chapter 6

The Rescue Mission

Chapter Framework:

-Old belief (before Untherapy): I do not matter. My only worth is derived from my ability to successfully support and fix other people. I am not allowed to have an opinion. I deserve to be abused. It is for my own good and the only way to keep me in line. Based on my sacrifice, I am earning a reward with God, which He will owe me at some undetermined point in the future.

-The Untherapy Perspective: Life is a non-zero-sum game. Everyone can win. My having more does not equal less for you. Lack is an illusion that challenges us to process our negative emotions and evolve our understanding. There is no glory in playing the martyr. Any belief that reinforces martyrdom is misguided and produces unnecessary misery. The Divine never stops reaching out to us, conspiring on our behalf to produce healing and growth. Even if we are actively working to thwart these blessings, we still end up receiving many of them. They are powerful proof of the true nature of life and the Divine.

"Fall seven times and stand up eight." –Japanese Proverb

Brad has been gradually restricting my contact with the outside world. I haven't had a friend in years, and he recently dropped the ultimatum that I could either have a relationship with my mom or have sex with him—but my choice would be final and permanent. Oh, how I wanted to choose my mom! But a good wife wouldn't dream of such nonsense. I haven't spoken to my family in months. No one knows what is going on behind our closed doors.

Celeste spends her days telling me stories from her past, playing with my babies (now two and four years old), and waiting for Brad to get home. I enjoy her company. It's nice to have a friend. Celeste reminds me of Delilah, and I immediately become her therapist. Once we've worked through her big childhood traumas, she reveals that her deepest desire is to have a child. Due to a mysterious medical condition I've never heard of, her doctor told her she can't have kids—ever. My heart breaks for her. Here I have these two beautiful children who are more than I ever deserved. Brad regularly reminds me, often in front of them, what a terrible mother I am and how I shouldn't be allowed to raise them. And here I have a third child on the way. It's almost too much. Wait, maybe it *is* too much. A perfect solution forms in my heart. I will give my baby to Celeste.

My understanding of the Godhead is that the bloodline follows the father. The methodical cadence of Dad's voice plodding through the Old Testament genealogies rings in my head. "And Nahshon begat Salma, and Salma begat Boaz, And Boaz begat Obed, and Obed begat Jesse," I Chron 2:11-12 (KJV). This child will stay under the protection of its Divine parent. Celeste will receive the blessing she's always wanted, and I won't risk ruining another child.

As soon as Brad is convinced that I'm serious, he gives me the go-ahead to make all the arrangements. Celeste starts attending our prenatal visits (much to midwife Susie's chagrin), and I buy a breast pump so she can start stimulating her hormones to produce a milk supply for the newborn. Every time my baby moves inside my swelling belly, I whisper loving reassurances that I will take care of him (I'm guessing it's a boy) for a few more months until he can go to the perfect parents for him.

A month passes, and Celeste is slipping out of the honeymoon phase. I don't hear crazy sex noises at all hours of the night anymore, and she's stopped using her breast pump. Without warning, she runs off to Nebraska. Brad is so distraught, he doesn't even demand sex from me while she's gone. I am more than happy to mother him in his distress. As he descends into debilitating depression and armed only with a phone book and fierce determination, I somehow manage to track her down at a seedy hotel outside of Omaha.

The manager begs me to come pick her up. "It sounds like an orgy in there 24/7," he says. "They're bothering the other guests." Brad is packed up and on his way in less than thirty minutes. Over a long weekend, he eventually convinces her to leave the old boyfriend she was hooking up with and return home.

Celeste comes back with a renewed determination to make this arrangement fun. One night, she and Brad approach me to act out her fantasy of watching him beat me up. The first blow lands square on my jaw with a jarring thud. I look him straight in the eyes as fire courses through my veins. I know something in this moment with absolute certainty. If we were in an actual fist fight, I would win.

"Is that all you've got?" I sneer.

He stumbles back and falls to the floor, sobbing. "What have I done? I've turned into my father!" he wails.

Celeste consoles him, and after a short pep talk, he resumes the beating. When she's had her fill, we sit in the garage while she smokes a cigarette. They tell me I'm going to be their love slave, and they describe the tattoo they've designed for me. The next morning, with yellow and blue bruises dotting my face, I tell them I don't think I can do this. I don't want to be their love slave. "Too late," Celeste responds brusquely. "This is what you signed up for." She grabs Brad's hand and they retire to the bedroom. In moments, their familiar sex noises assault my senses once again. I sink into the couch, numb with defeat.

The shrill ring of the phone startles me out of my haze. It's Brad's older sister, Rosie. She still holds a grudge for my mishandling of the Delilah rape debacle six years ago, so I'm not surprised at the curt tone she takes as she demands to speak to her brother. Her lack of decorum, coupled with the events of the previous several weeks, have strained my pregnant mind to the breaking point. A hard lump of resentment deep in my gut prompts me to reckless action. I pull the pin and lob the grenade ever so gently into the phone. "Oh, he's busy having sex with his girlfriend in the bedroom. Want me to take a message?"

I hold the phone away from my ear for a solid ninety seconds while she lets off the first layer of steam. Now that the seal is broken, the questions come hard and fast. What am I allowing? When did this start? How are the kids coping? Like flood waters breaching a levy, the truth comes tumbling out. I tell her the whole story of how Celeste joined our family, ending with my plan to give my baby up to her for adoption.

The line grows quiet. In a measured voice, she quotes Psalm 127:3 (NASB): "Behold, children are a gift of the LORD, the fruit of the womb is a reward." After a long pause, she adds, "That is a gift from God that is meant for *you*, not some slut that's banging my brother."

As if God Himself had spoken, these words snap me out of a stupor. With a burst of insight, I hang up and call my dad. In an ongoing effort to alienate me from my family, Brad has recently enjoyed making me write carefully curated letters to my parents that reflect my absolute submission. Three weeks ago, Dad showed up at my doorstep unannounced to plead with me. After a brief conversation in the driveway, I sent him away on the six-hour return trip.

He answers on the first ring. "Hey, Dad, you know how you've been worried about me? Yeah, what you said would happen is happening. I need to get out of here…FAST."

Without hesitation, he replies, "I'll be there in the morning."

After Brad and Celeste go to bed, I surreptitiously pack a small bag for each kid and one for myself. I lie awake all night on our floor pallet, their little bodies curled trustingly around me. I rise early to write a note. "Dear Brad and Celeste, I need a break. I'll only be gone for a couple weeks. There's leftover chili in the fridge. See you soon, Love, A." I grab the kids and slip out the front door before anyone else wakes up.

Moving back in with my parents at twenty-five years old is an eye-opener. The rules and restrictions of my childhood are not so noticeable, and the nightly Bible studies soothe my tired soul. They have a small guest house where Gideon, Hannah, and I have our privacy. My two little sisters, Ruth and Abigail, are homeschooled teenagers now. I tutor them and borrow their car to run errands. Mom bakes bread and cooks delicious meals from the garden, all the while listening graciously to the endless waterfall of overdue words I finally get to express.

As days turn into weeks, my intention to return home gradually fades. Dad encourages me to talk to a divorce lawyer. Frankly, I'm shocked at this suggestion, since he's the one who taught me the evils of ending a marriage. He explains that there are exemptions and offers to pay for it. I temporarily suspend my decision in order to focus on a more pressing issue.

I've had exactly one month to change the narrative with the growing life inside me. "You are *my* baby," I reassure him. "I promise to take care of you and never let you go. I'm sorry for almost giving you away." I worry that my mental state has damaged him, and I pray he will be fully formed and healthy.

Precisely on my due date, Mom and a local midwife help me give birth in my little sister's bed (she is away at summer camp). I was right! He is a boy, and I get to choose his name all by myself. Four-year-old big brother Gideon gets to cut the cord. At ten pounds, eleven ounces, Luke is perfect in every way. My whole being breathes an epic sigh of relief. The midwife shows me the hard ridge of calcification bordering my placenta. She has only seen this in mothers who smoke during their whole pregnancy or those who experience severe stress.

I decide to move forward with divorce proceedings. Brad comes up for an initial hearing and wants to see the kids. Dad is not allowing him on the property (which is understandable), so I agree to meet him in town, where the local fair is underway. We let the kids ride ponies and play carnival games while we talk. It's been five months since I was physically near him, and it feels like all those terrible memories are just a bad movie I never want to watch again.

A beautiful sunset spreads orange and pink hues across the happy families milling through the fairgrounds. With the sweet smell of cotton candy and funnel cakes wafting by, Brad pours out his heart. He tells me how much he misses me and how Celeste was a mistake. He wants our family back together. He never stopped loving me and can't forget how special I am to him. He promises that she's gone, and he won't ever ask me to do anything I don't want again.

"And what about swinging?" I ask.

"That's over," he assures me. "We won't ever be swingers again." I am all he needs. Won't I please, please just come back home so we can have our life together again? He reaches for my hand, and I let him hold it. My lonely, aching heart yearns for this fairy tale. He is my husband. He is the only one who can make all my dreams come true. In the gossamer twilight, we stroll by a man I recognize—it's my lawyer. He gives me a meaningful side-eye as we make our way through the crowd. I decide that he doesn't understand loneliness.

It takes me a couple weeks to process this new development. At my next appointment with the lawyer, he reads my mind like a fortune teller. He's seen it a thousand times, he says. He knows I've already made up my mind.

I sit down with Dad to let him know. We arrange ourselves cross-legged on his bed as I explain the miracle God has performed to heal and restore my family. Always the stoic, I expect my dad to express an appropriate level of subdued joy at my Divine victory. Instead, for only the second time in my life, I witness tears rolling down his face. He begs me not to go, but I will not be dissuaded from the will of the Almighty for my life. Brad moves us back home later that week.

I bubble over with excitement on the trip home, but as I step in the front door, an uneasy feeling prompts a trepidatious pause. The kids run on ahead, eager to play with toys they haven't seen in months. As I enter the living room, I see it. There on the floor, not five feet in front of me, is a shoe; actually, a sandal—the goddess style that straps up your ankle. Celeste's sandal. That old familiar feeling upends me—I am falling, falling, grabbing at the air. Brad notices my gaze.

My breath finally returns. "Is she still here?!" My incredulous tone sounds at once angry and sad.

He rushes to reassure me that she's almost moved out and I won't have to see her. He's taking the last of her things to her later today. I point out that somehow, he failed to mention his ongoing contact with her. I was under the impression she left months ago.

"It *is* over," he insists, but I don't believe him. And now I feel trapped. I just burned the only bridge I had when I made my dad cry.

Within the first six months of being back, I go from hopeful to helpless. Celeste is still in the picture, and when I demand that Brad stop spending time at her place, he reveals that she's pregnant. Turns out the medical condition that rendered her barren was borrowed from her favorite soap opera, as were most of the stories she told me. He's also angry that I ever left and holds it against me every chance he gets. He starts hitting me, not for fantasy reasons this time, but as an outlet for his anger. His depressive episodes are getting longer and more severe, and he adds threats of suicide to his repertoire.

One day, upon returning home from work, he removes his shoes just inside the front door. When I inquire, he demonstrates how to sanitize the soles before putting them away in the closet. Every few days, he repeats this strange behavior. He supervises the first few cleanings and thereafter lets me do it myself, always inspecting to verify it was done correctly.

Several weeks pass, and he finally reveals that he has recently discovered a suppressed childhood memory of being molested by his stepfather. As a way of processing the abuse, he has been frequenting the viewing booths at local porn shops to hook up with other men. The floors there are unsanitary, for obvious reasons. Hence the need to meticulously clean his shoes. When I ask him if it's helping, he says, "Sometimes." When I ask him if that's why he and Delilah were sexually active as children, he says their "games" were always her idea. He doesn't know if she was molested. When I ask if he is using a condom, he hits me in the back of the head with the unopened can of Sprite he is holding. The force of the blow explodes the can open, spraying sticky liquid over the whole room. I barely notice the knot on the back of my head. I rush to clean up the mess, making a note to care less about my health and safety from now on.

Brad's suicidal tendencies become a normal part of his cycles. At least once a month, he disappears, calling every few minutes to detail exactly how he is going to kill himself. When he finally stops calling, I sink back in the bed, hoping this time he will go through with it. Everything would be so much easier, I tell myself. But he won't. I know he won't. It would be too easy. That's just not how my life works.

It is at these lowest moments, when I've spent every last drop of energy I possess, and my little kids are crying for me in the other room, that I feel inexplicable comfort deep in my soul. Every time my heart hits rock bottom, I know that it will get better. I have no proof and no understanding of how this will happen. I just know. Brad will heal, we will be happy, and everything will magically turn into cupcakes and roses. Then I will get to do what I've always wanted to do: help other people who are struggling. It makes no sense, but it keeps me going. And at this point, I'll take any shred of hope I can get.

He's ready to start swinging again. He insists that I at least owe him that much. I hold out for two more months, but each day, the pressure is a little worse. He has started hitting me most days, but only on my head and abdomen, where the bruises won't show. One night while we're watching TV, I unexpectedly break down sobbing at a diaper commercial. A pregnancy test eliminates any doubt: I'm having another baby.

As with the previous pregnancies, Brad's sexual appetite kicks into overdrive. I finally capitulate. We frequent bars and night clubs for hook ups, but we have even more luck at sex clubs. As we become regulars at several local establishments, Brad and I are now an active part of the swinging community. Unlike regular bars, women are never groped or dominated in these settings. The rules of each club clearly define consent and encourage couples to work through issues of trust, boundary-setting, and communication ahead of time. Only a handful of single males are granted entrance on any given night. Bouncers stand by, ready to remove any man who bothers a woman in any way. Everyone knows the unspoken rule: inside these walls, women have all the power. For our purposes, this arrangement is perfect, and in my desire to please Brad, the irony is completely lost on me.

I consider myself un-rapeable. It has been so long since my body belonged to me that I can no longer imagine a scenario where I would have an opinion about what is being done to it. Brad selects a woman he wants, and I work my magic to seduce the couple into a private room so he can have his way with her. All I must do is keep the husband occupied until Brad is finished.

Experienced couples have already defined their boundaries and rules before any "play" commences. A short conversation at the outset avoids any awkward mishaps. This boundary talk harkens back to my dating days, except there are four people, and the rules are set by everyone *but* me. The most common boundary is no kissing. It's too intimate. Brad has set this rule for our relationship as well. These men can touch me all over and put their body parts in any opening they desire, but heaven forbid they would touch their lips to mine. That is reserved for the sanctity of marriage. Sometimes the wife is into other women, and she and I put on a show for the men. This is the only time I can relax and enjoy myself. Women are so gentle and attentive by comparison.

It's a tiny oasis of pleasure amid masterminding Brad's experience, but I never let myself get so lost in the moment that I forget why we're really here.

Sometimes we find a newbie couple to play with. I become adept at discerning the ones with adventurous, carefree energy. They have the fewest boundaries, and Brad usually ends up getting more of what he wants. I learn to predict when Brad is wanting to go to the sex club because for a few days prior, he stops hitting me where others would see the bruises.

I give birth to my fourth child three weeks after my twenty-seventh birthday. Midwife Susie needed quite a few questions answered before she would take me on again, but thankfully she has forgiven my poor judgment and supports me beautifully through yet another home birthing experience. Susie has become a therapist of sorts. I never reveal the truth of my existence to her, but she has nurtured and supported me through the toughest parts of my life for over six years.

This is the only birth my mom does not attend. I miss her. Once again, I am sure of the gender ahead of time: it feels like another boy. I've gone three for three on my guesses, so there's no reason to doubt my intuition. Ella arrives in defiant triumph. Her fierce spirit knows what she wants and isn't afraid to go after it. She is so unlike me, even as an infant, that I marvel at how she could've come from my body. I decide she must have needed that determination to thrive in the toxic environment of my womb.

My life continues as a blur: raising four young children and waiting on my increasingly complicated husband's every whim. Weekends are the hardest. Without work to keep him occupied, Brad locks me in the bedroom for hours at a time demanding that I placate the monster of his ever-increasing sexual appetite. Big brother Gideon watches his younger siblings as well as any eight-year-old could be expected to. I get strep throat at least once a month, but I tough it out and always recover without having to break down and go to the doctor. Sometimes when Brad hugs me, I grit my teeth so hard, it blurs my vision.

One particularly gloomy Saturday night, Brad is in the mood to have some fun. I've just recovered from my most recent bout with strep and want nothing more than a warm shower and a long night's sleep. One look at his stone-faced expression, and I scurry to my closet for a sexy outfit. We argue all the way to the club, which is more of an exercise in how many ways I can apologize for existing. As we sit in the parking lot, my body glues itself to the seat, too exhausted to move. Finally, I peel myself out of the car and head for the front door. I will myself to reach for the handle, but even as I pull, Brad is railing at me to put up or shut up. Going home at this point would be certain disaster, so I decide to gamble on the club. Maybe some woman here is looking for what he has to offer. We spend the first hour milling around, greeting the regulars, and scoping for new talent. Brad is at the tipping point of succumbing to ennui, and I'm moments from conceding defeat, when it happens.

****

If this chapter stirred some strong emotions about the harder parts of your life, especially the cycles that seem to constantly pull you back into harmful relationships or addictive behaviors, I'd love to offer you the Chapter 6 Study Guide, which delves deeper into these issues. Download it at theuntherapist.com/chapter6 to learn more about how you can cooperate with the natural support of the Divine to rescue yourself.

Chapter 7

Oh, There You Are

Chapter Framework:

-Old belief (before Untherapy): Life is a game of chance controlled by the most powerful men in the room. I am at the mercy of my circumstances, which usually means life is hard and I am miserable. When good things happen, I am only allowed to accept them if someone outside myself (God or a man) gives me permission.

-The Untherapy Perspective: We are each the main character of our own unique life. This is equally true for every human. Life is meant to be enjoyed. As we intentionally release our fearful need to force and control outcomes, we can trust that our best choices will lead us to what we most desire. Even when we are in active resistance against the Divine, we are still being met with opportunities to heal, learn, and evolve. What we most need and want is constantly finding us.

"To be fully seen by somebody, then, and be loved anyhow – this is a human offering that can border on miraculous." –Elizabeth Gilbert

Brad and I are camped out in the main room where we have a good view of any new arrivals. There's a hubbub as a woman enters, encircled by a group of doting admirers. She is older, tall, and mildly overweight, with dark hair and eyes. Despite her plain appearance, she carries herself like she's queen of the world. These men are fawning over her, vying for her attention. You can smell the testosterone from here. She settles into a spot of her liking while one of the men in her entourage slumps in a nearby chair, unceremoniously facing away from her. He pulls his baseball cap low over his eyes as if preparing for a mid-afternoon siesta. I'm struck by the juxtaposition of these two figures and decide he must've happened in at the same time as this group but surely isn't related to it.

Brad's eyes gleam as his gaze rests on his prey. He turns to me, his voice dripping with desire. "I want her." Really? I don't say it out loud, but this woman looks like the opposite of the young, thin, fresh-faced beauty he normally selects.

I know better than to question or hesitate, so without delay, I part the sea of leering eyes and approach the queen. Her name is Karen, and she's here with her husband. She motions toward the disinterested napper.

"Wait, he's your husband?" My voice sounds more incredulous than I had planned.

"Oh, he's just tired," she responds dismissively.

I look around at the four other men panting at her feet. What is it with this woman? Never mind that now—I introduce her to Brad and immediately recognize the mutual attraction. Bingo! I allow a silent sigh of relief. My night is saved. I reach for her husband's hand, rousing him from his stupor, and ask him to help me clear a private room. He complies with what feels like genuine support. Once we've emptied the room, I thank him, and he turns to leave.

"Wait!" I insist. "This room is for us!"

His baffled expression quickly morphs into excitement as Brad and Karen push past us to claim the bed. Husband and I gladly take the couch with an unspoken understanding that our spouses are the complicated ones. His name is Tom, and as we tentatively arrange ourselves on the couch, I notice that Brad and Karen are *kissing*! I feel a surge of excitement. He is so distracted by this woman; I sense a rare moment of freedom for myself.

After a bit of maneuvering, I'm able to balance on the narrow couch, facing Tom, straddling his lap. With the muffled happy sounds of our spouses in the background, our eyes meet for the first time. I'm struck with an overwhelming desire to kiss him. It's against the rules. I feel myself succumbing to the irresistible urge. I glance over my shoulder to ensure Brad's attention is consumed by Karen. Then I go for it. The instant our lips meet, I feel a surge of energy as a jolt of electricity passes between us. I draw back in surprise.

"Oh! There you are!" The words fall out of my mouth before I know what I'm saying.

His crystal-blue eyes return my gaze with a knowing look. We kiss again. And again. For a moment, I forget about real life. There is no pain, no fear, no getting beaten up for incorrectly plating my husband's dinner. There is only this. This moment of absolute perfection.

There is a knock at the door. Another couple wants to join. I shoot daggers in the direction of the bed, praying they will choose privacy. No such luck. Karen invites them in, quickly decides they aren't what she hoped for, and at Brad's suggestion of "Anne-Lise will take care of them," passes them off to me. As I entertain the husband, Tom sits to my left, watching. I don't want to do this right now. I reach for Tom's hand. He takes mine and squeezes it reassuringly. Soon the wife is jealous enough to shut down their night. The moment they leave, I sink back into Tom.

By the time Brad and Karen have had their fill, I am smitten. Tom has handled my body with a level of care and respect that I cannot fathom. Brad is uncharacteristically preoccupied with Karen, creating enough space for me to have a moment of privacy with Tom. He wraps his arms around me, buries his head in my hair, and whispers, "Thank you. I'm not usually this aggressive. I hope I didn't overstep your boundaries." I breathe deeply and lock this moment into my permanent memory bank. It is a feeling I want to remember forever.

On the car ride home, I nervously attempt to conceal my excitement. I cannot un-feel what I felt. I cannot un-know what I know. Someone saw me for who I am. Someone saw *me*. My self has spontaneously expanded to a new, larger size that doesn't fit in the previous container. With a sense of foreboding, I scan my repertoire of survival skills. Nothing. Blessedly, I quickly realize there's no need to worry…yet.

Brad is so taken with Karen; she is all he can talk about. Her touch, her voice, her breasts, her moves. I remember the doting entourage that arrived with her. Whatever drug she's passing out, apparently my husband has taken a dose. I'm careful to conceal my disdain, but I really don't get it. She's so…plain! A pang of jealousy sears my heart. With all the effort I put forth to please him, he goes for someone like *that*?

Before I can descend any further into frustration, I am placated by my own afterglow. When Brad forgets to ask me how my night went, I breathe an audible sigh of relief. This has *never* happened before. For the first time, I have space to process my own thoughts and feelings without being required to expose every minute detail to Brad's hyper-critical eye. I am aware that I've dodged the ultimate bullet.

Once we are home and I've provided the obligatory post-sex-club sex, I lie next to my snoring husband, wide awake. Part of me feels like I already know Tom, like I have always known him. I remind myself that this will never happen again. There's no point being open with Brad about it. I'll only get myself beaten. It's not lying. It's just omission of irrelevant details. Next time there will be a new couple. It was nice while it lasted, but it's out of my hands, and it's over. Back to reality. I decide I will allow myself to keep this one pleasant memory in the sea of misery that is my normal life. I deserve that much.

The next day, when Brad suggests we call Tom and Karen to arrange another meeting, I feign apathy. I pray that I've concealed the thrill of excitement that jolted through my body the moment he mentioned it. They come over after the kids are asleep, and the four of us share our king-size bed. As so many times before, I engage in sex with another man while my own husband lies inches from me, consumed with this man's wife. But this is not like other times. This feels *good.* I find myself lost in the moment again and again.

My efforts to remain vigilant and facilitate Brad's pleasure become futile as I am swept away in the pleasure and connection I feel with Tom. Over and over, my body responds with waves of rolling orgasm I didn't realize I was even capable of. I decide that since I don't have words for these inexplicable feelings, I am not required to articulate them to Brad later. I justify my behavior by reminding myself that I am not hiding anything. I am out in the open, in plain sight. Anything Brad wants to know is right here for him to observe.

Tom and Karen start coming over any evening they are available. I am relieved and reassured when Brad does not focus on my actions, but instead continues to fall deeper under the spell that Karen has cast upon him. Even calling Tom to arrange our meetings leaves me weak in the knees. One time, we decide to count how many times we can have sex in a row. We stop at nineteen, not because we are done, but because Brad and Karen decide we are too much and demand that we take a break.

Within a few weeks, Tom and I have dragged an extra twin mattress into the bathroom to give Brad and Karen some privacy. Then we move to the back porch. After a month, we are swapping houses. As soon as the kids are down for the night, I head to Tom's house while Karen heads to mine. I still feel a profound sense of loyalty to my marriage, and I vow to honestly answer any questions Brad asks about my experiences with Tom, provided I can find the words for them. He is none the wiser, caught up in the delights of his new conquest. I am grateful beyond words for every chance to be with Tom. I always treat it as if it is my last. Sex with Tom is easy, fun, pleasurable, consensual, and mutually gratifying. These are all new experiences for me, and I consider them a rare gift that just might be God's reward for all my years of hard work.

As a bonus, Brad hits me less frequently and more intentionally. We are pretty much limited to blows to the head, since those bruises can't be seen. Sometimes I still need to be put back in my place, but we can't have Tom and Karen finding out our little secret. By now, Brad has thoroughly convinced me that all husbands beat their wives. It's part of the role they are supposed to play as the dominant partner. It's just one of those grown-up secrets no one talks about.

After four months of swapping like this, Tom and Karen reveal that they've decided to get a divorce. It's strictly for financial reasons, and it's been coming for a while. They've been trying to make it work for over fifteen years, but she simply can't handle the insecurity of being married to a self-employed spouse. He started a drywall and paint contracting business right out of high school and has never worked for anyone else. She has a stable income as a high-level manager at an insurance company. Tom offhandedly remarks that she wouldn't even have that job if he hadn't paid to put her through school.

Either way, it means our relationship with Tom and Karen is over. There simply isn't a way to maintain the sanctity of our marriage and the extra level of trust and communication necessary on all sides when the other couple is no longer together. I am devastated, but I suck it up hard and pretend it's no big deal. I knew going in that I had no control over how long this would last. Brad acts devastated, and I'm overcome with the urge to mock his heartbreak. I barely manage to reel myself in, but I placate him by bringing home a new couple for us. They are underwhelming. I mentally flog myself for having gotten so attached to Tom.

Two weeks have passed when late on a Tuesday afternoon, I get a random phone call from Tom. This used to be par for the course. He and I were the ones who coordinated all the liaisons. But all that is behind us now. I'm expecting Brad home from work any moment, and I'm nervous to get off the phone quickly before he catches me in an unauthorized conversation.

Tom's voice sounds both confident and incredulous. "I'm helping Karen move into her new house today. I'm dropping off the last load, and guess who just pulled up…with their overnight bag?"

I'm so confused. Why is he calling, and how would I know who is showing up at Karen's new house tonight? His voice brings me back to the moment. "It's Brad. Brad is here. I think he's planning on staying with her."

I drop the phone. Once again, I am falling, falling, falling. But just before I hit the ground, something inside me surges me back into an upright position. I can feel my blood boiling through my veins as I dial Brad's number. "Where are you?" I demand. This is the first time I have ever called him out. It feels foreign to vocalize emotion to him.

His voice sounds uncertain, almost pleading. "I'm going to stay with Karen. You just keep the house and the kids in order. I will be around some."

"You want me to *wait* for you?" I'm gobsmacked. After a brief pause, it hits me. "You're scared of her, aren't you? You are more afraid of losing her than of losing me." I've poked the bear, and rather than scared, I feel indignant. How dare he? After all I've done for him!

"I am not afraid of *any* woman," comes his angry retort. "Just be a good wife and we won't have any problems."

"Come home now or don't come home at all." The ultimatum shoots out of my mouth like a bullet from a gun. I don't wait for him to respond. I hang up the phone, sit down on the couch, and wait. I wait all night, watching the front door. I fluctuate between blessed relief ("Does this mean I could actually get a break?") and exquisite resentment ("Is this my reward for a life of endless torture?"). The enduring hope that had always faithfully appeared when I hit rock bottom seems to taunt me with enervating clarity. *He will never change, and you just wasted the best years of your life on a dead-end project that was doomed for failure before it ever started.* I'm pretty sure God just died.

The next day, Tom asks to come over. He has never met my kids, and I don't know how to address their dad's absence, so I tell him to come after bedtime. We sit on the front porch to talk. After about an hour, a local police officer shows up to kick Tom off the property. There has been a complaint from the owner of the home (even though the house is also in my name), so he is no longer allowed on the premises, under threat of criminal trespass charges. Tom and I move our lawn chairs to the driveway of the vacant house across the street and continue our conversation.

I am talking to Tom, really talking, for the first time. Even though I have been sharing my body with him for months, it was always in the context of swinging. I was always Brad's wife who had sex with Tom, ostensibly so Brad and Karen could have their time together. I was ever vigilant to keep things superficial, and although Tom shared his own life details freely and openly, I was careful never to reveal anything that would cast Brad or our marriage in a negative light. Now I am something else. I belong to no one. I float in an in-between that is both exhilarating and terrifying. Who sets my rules? How do I keep myself in line? What am I allowed to feel and think? Who is my God? The last time I had this feeling was the brief window of freedom when I left home for college at seventeen. At thirty years old, I don't even trust myself enough to order my own meal at a restaurant. I am a total stranger in my own life.

After just a few nights of sitting with Tom in the driveway across the street, my fabric of tightly held beliefs is beginning to unravel. I still haven't told him the secrets of my marriage, but I have been shocked at his level of emotional intelligence and ability to predict behavior. Tom tells me how this whole breakup is going to go down. As he explains Karen's patterns and guesses at Brad's responses, he hits the nail on the head again and again. Without either of us realizing what is happening, Tom's insight is systematically dismantling a lifetime of carefully constructed rules. I clung to these rules like my very life depended on it: don't talk back, don't say no, don't think for yourself, don't hesitate, don't question, fear Brad like you fear God.

Listening to Tom share his faith in Divine power, I wonder for the first time if maybe God doesn't hate me. What if I didn't have to spend my entire existence trying to prove that I am worthy of whatever shred of love Jesus could spare for my despicable soul today? What if I, as a woman, am not, in fact, a lesser being who requires constant abuse just to stay in line? What if I could like myself the way Tom likes himself? He doesn't make it look dangerous.

From this perspective, I begin to see the absurd nature of my own thoughts. Nothing is sacred: not my marriage, not Brad's behavior, not my carefully curated words and actions. My years of herculean effort pile up in useless ruin against the hope that they would someday magically be rewarded with a spontaneous miracle of happily ever after.

The following weekend, I'm ready to introduce Tom to my kids. He's a genuine friend now, and I want to be able to spend time with him beyond our late-night lawn chair conversations. Gideon is now nine, Hannah is seven, Luke is five, and Ella is three. We take them to a nearby McDonald's, and they happily consume fries and milkshakes while running back and forth to the playscape.

I'm halfway through my burger when the scene becomes too much for me. Here's this man, being a friend, sharing life with me, and he isn't asking me for anything. He hasn't even mentioned sex or so much as made a pass at me since we've been talking. He's joking with my kids, genuinely enjoying their delight at the unexpected outing, and it's all way too overwhelmingly perfect. I can't do this. There must be a catch. The other shoe is about to drop, and my frayed nervous system cannot withstand another betrayal. I feel my body falling as I launch into a full-blown panic attack. I'm usually pretty successful at controlling them, but this one has caught me with my guard down. I brace myself against the edge of the table while I gasp for air.

Tom gently pats my back while reassuring the kids. Once I am calm enough to speak, I launch into a self-deprecating diatribe. I apologize for ruining our outing, for my weakness, for my existence. I pause for a breath, not knowing what to expect. I've never lost my head around him before. Tom puts his hand reassuringly on my arm, gazes into my eyes, and says firmly, "If this is your way of trying to get rid of me, you need to just be honest with me. If you don't want me to be here, I'll go. But I will *not* tolerate you beating yourself up like this. You need to decide which it will be...right now."

I am speechless. I'm not even sure what those words mean, but I know I don't want him to go. Backed into a corner with nothing left to lose, I slowly reply, "I think I need to tell you something." I take a deep breath and continue, "I was the one who replaced the toilet." A couple months prior, when we were in the thick of our full swap arrangements, I had asked Tom for advice on how to replace a toilet. I told him Brad had prompted me to ask because the toilet in the kid's bathroom had started leaking. The truth was, it had been leaking for over a year, and it was getting unmanageable. Knowing Tom's construction background, I had concocted the idea of asking for his advice under the guise of getting the info for Brad. Brad was always prideful about being perceived as the man of the house, so I had to do all the house maintenance in secret. I would mow the lawn quickly during the workday so the neighbors wouldn't notice, fix the roof under the cover of night, and replace the toilet while giving him full credit.

Once I begin telling Tom the truth about my life, I can't stop. As I pick up momentum, jumping from one shocking revelation to another, I know two things with absolute certainty: 1) It feels amazing to be honest, and 2) This is the last conversation I will ever have with Tom. No way he's recovering from this. One story rolls into another, each more exposing than the last. I start with the inside scoop on events Tom experienced since we met. He feels justified to finally have proof of what he had begun to suspect—something wasn't right in our marriage. With his encouragement, I continue reaching deeper into the shameful places I've never revealed to another living soul.

With each confession, I know I am severing any ties that I could possibly have with this man in the future. But the pressure of years of unspoken secrets has taken over. They escape in dark clusters like swarms of bats stirred from their resting place deep in a hidden cave. It's beyond my control to stop them. I string the stories together with, "There's so much more" and "Oh, it gets way worse." Tom nods encouragingly, utters a periodic "wow!", and swallows hard at each new revelation.

Apart from a few short pauses to handle the kids, we spend the next thirteen hours in a confessional of epic proportion. By now it is 1:00 a.m., and we're in my bedroom. With the last words of the last story uttered, I sink to the floor in sheer exhaustion. "And now you know everything. That's all the secrets I've never told anyone." I bow my head, feeling only the absence of feeling, as I wait for Tom to leave.

He gathers me up in his muscular arms and helps me to the bed, sitting down beside me and gently taking my hand. "I think it's time for me to share my faith with you," he says. A brief description of his spiritual understanding introduces me to the foreign concepts of grace and forgiveness by a Divine power who isn't angry and vindictive. He leads me in what he calls "The Sinner's Prayer", which, despite the scary name, feels more like a metaphysical release of a lifetime of burden. And then, without effort or strain, I initiate the most gratifying, present-in-my-body sex of my entire life. As we lie in the afterglow, bodies wrapped into one being, a solitary thought floats luxuriously across my blissful mind: "So *this* is what all the fuss is about."

****

If you feel like your life is just a random string of chance happenings, some good but mostly bad, may I strongly suggest that you download the Study Guide for Chapter 7? In it, you will find ways to connect with the true nature of life and the Divine. I am confident you will come away from this work with a renewed sense of optimism about your future. Find it at theuntherapist.com/chapter7.

Chapter 8

Space to Heal

Chapter Framework:

-Old belief (before Untherapy): Sometimes you get lucky, and situations or people temporarily rescue you from your misery. When life gets too easy, just wait…the other shoe is sure to drop. There's always a catch. People only love me for how much I can help them. I am a failure. I am incompetent. I do not deserve to be happy. Fun and ease are confusing traps that must be navigated with even greater care than struggle and striving.

-The Untherapy Perspective: Desire is proof of deserve. When we want something, we can recognize that this desire is directly connected to the ideal next steps for us. If we acknowledge our desires and pursue them with intention and consistency, we can release our attachment to specific outcomes, knowing that innate course corrections will continue to perfect our path toward a more gratifying life. The supportive nature of life continually brings us opportunities and relationships that are meant to help us heal, grow, and thrive. The more we lean into this truth, the more our reality will reflect this supportive paradigm.

"The only meaningful thing we can offer one another is love. Not advice, not questions about our choices, not suggestions for the future, just love." – Glennon Doyle

I wake up the next morning to a shifted consciousness. As I open my eyes and snuggle deeper into Tom's arms, I am overwhelmed with a deep longing to make him happy. The void that was left by releasing so much shame all at once gives me entirely too much space for my own comfort. I must fill it by doing something helpful. As I get up to make Tom a cup of coffee, I am gripped with fear that Brad is spying on me. Has he been watching the house? Will he call the cops again when he sees Tom's truck parked out front? I push the thought away for the moment. I bring Tom his coffee in bed, and as he rouses himself to sit up, I notice tears forming in his eyes. I frantically search my mind for what I've done wrong. Is it the cup? Did he want cream? Sugar?

"Thank you," his voice catches through his tears. "In all my years of being married, my wife never brought me a drink, not even a glass of water when I was sick. Thank you."

My panic is replaced with a rush of relief. "Wow!" I tell myself, "This is going to be *easy*!"

That night after he's home from work, Tom and I discuss plans for the future. He tells me he doesn't want me to feel any pressure to decide one way or another, but he's thought it through. "I don't want to date around or waste time on anyone else. I want you. Do whatever you want with that."

A new feeling of floating in the great unknown of cosmic possibilities has captured my imagination. I am untethered from the past, with all its rules that kept me small and fearful. I allow myself to daydream about a life with Tom: a life where I am wanted, cherished, and valued. It feels way too good to be true, and yet, here he is—holding me, talking to me, seeing me, wanting me, choosing me.

What do I want? He is asking me. He keeps saying, "No pressure. I want you to do what *you* want. I would rather your answer be a 'no' than for you to do something you don't want to." I am unsure what he means by this. It is an altogether new concept, but there is a tangible sense of freedom in the idea.

He confesses his worst fear. By the end of his marriage to Karen, their connection was so toxic that he had become verbally abusive. "I don't think I would ever treat you like that, but it became almost a habit for me," he explains. "I want you to know up front that, as careful as I want to be, there is a chance I might do it to you."

"But you won't hit me, right?" I quickly counter.

"No, I am absolutely sure I would never hit you. If I had that in me, I would've done it to Karen, and I never did."

"Great!" comes my lighthearted reply. "I can totally handle verbal abuse. That's easy!"

We talk about the kids. His only son with Karen (adopted by Tom when the boy was two years old) is a senior in high school and very self-sufficient. He'll be off to college in less than a year, so Tom's parenting years are basically over. Does he want to start all over again with four kids, ages three to nine? With all the talk of space and autonomy, I bravely assert that I am a package deal. If he isn't ready to commit to the kids, I'm out.

"Give me twenty-four hours," he says. "I don't want to make this decision lightly."

Tom comes back the next day with a "yes." He's also found several houses he wants me to look at. We must get away from anything Brad has control over. He shows me his favorite one first, and as we step through the front door into the spacious family room, I remark, "This is too big! We don't need all this space!"

He turns to me, laughing. "Have you seen how many kids we have?"

In less than two weeks, we've moved into that brand new, spacious two-story in a great neighborhood a few miles away. Tom is absolutely brimming with practical ideas and ways to solve everyday problems in the household. He talks with me about setting an intentionally supportive atmosphere for the kids. We keep the stereo tuned to a radio station that bills itself as "positive and encouraging." We eat meals together around the table. He makes time every evening for us to all pile on the couch and watch funny videos and lighthearted movies as a family. We hire a babysitter to help with the kids and the housework while I work part-time as a personal assistant for a woman who encourages and nurtures my new-found autonomy. We get a minivan so everyone can ride together in the same vehicle.

The kids start relaxing and opening up. After a couple weeks, Gideon, now a fourth grader, comes home from school one day and remarks, "Mom, you're never crying when I get home anymore. I like it when you're happy!"

A few days later, we are sharing a family meal when Luke (age five) casually comments, "Mom, remember that one time when Papa (their nickname for Brad) took you in the bedroom with that big knife?"

I freeze like a deer in the headlights.

"Yeah," adds Hannah (age seven) matter-of-factly, "we thought he was gonna kill you."

I rack my brain to think of which time they are referring to. There are far too many of these occurrences for me to know which one, and I just pray they don't remember any others. We talk about how I am safe and happy now, and I breathe a sigh of relief when the discussion shifts to a friend's upcoming birthday party.

Tom helps me work out a 50/50 visitation plan with Brad to have the kids on alternating weeks. I'm sure Brad agrees just to avoid having to pay child support, but Tom reassures me that Karen wouldn't let anything bad happen to the kids.

On the weeks we are alone, Tom and I stay up late into the night getting to know each other. We share our favorite music with each other, and he shows me videos of preachers that inspire him. I rub his feet while he listens to my stories. Brad never liked his feet rubbed, and since Tom works construction, his feet always hurt. It becomes our nightly ritual: I verbally process my past while digging out the knots in his feet. When I stumble upon a particularly painful memory, he reminds me to go easy.

As our bodies detoxify from years of chronic stress and unhappiness, we both experience the movement of bizarre physical symptoms through our bodies, from flu-like to severe allergies, unexplained headaches, shooting pain, numbness, and tingling in various body parts. Not surprisingly, I never again have a bout of strep throat. All those years of poisoning my body have been cleansed out of my throat as I freely speak my truth.

At Tom's prompting, I make the first doctor's appointment of my life and get diagnosed with chronic anxiety and depression. I begin taking two different medications, my first experience with prescription drugs. Within a couple weeks, my moods level off and I experience an improvement in my overall sense of well-being. After three months, the excruciating pain Tom has endured from years of plantar fasciitis is completely gone. Before we got together, he was getting injections straight into the heel every few months to manage the pain. Now he can stand up straight out of bed first thing in the morning with no pain.

We begin to attend a local nondenominational mega church where we can get the kids some extra support and where we can blend in without being noticed. One Sunday morning during the worship service, I am crying my eyes out, asking God to show me what to do about the kids. I am worried about them being with Brad. They always return from his house acting agitated and distant. It takes most of the week for them to settle down and relax, and then it's time to go back. I still don't feel like I deserve to be their mom. So many years of failing them has left me feeling directionless and incapable.

With hands raised and eyes closed, swept away by the lilting music, I pour my heart out to this new God-figure I've only known for a few months: this gentler, more loving entity that forgives and renews. As I'm praying, a voice whispers in my ear, "*You* take care of those kids." My eyes fly open, and I glance around in alarm to see who said that. Tom is lost in his own experience next to me, eyes closed, swaying to the music. I suddenly realize this is a message from God. It is the first tangible positive moment of Divine connection I have ever consciously experienced. Somehow, inexplicably, the Creator of all the Universe thinks I should be the one to raise my kids. How do you argue with that?

After I explain my spiritual experience to Tom, he says it's time to put a plan in place to secure custody of the kids. Neither Brad nor I have filed any legal paperwork yet. I know I should be proactive. The first one to file sets the precedent, but I still fear breaking the "God hates divorce" rule. For now, Tom and I decide to take steps to clean up our image so we can ensure the best possible outcome. Without hesitation, and to my surprise, he informs me he will quit drinking. He loves tequila, and he has no doubt Karen will try to use that fact against us in the custody battle. We also decide that, for appearances, it is probably best that we not be living together. We don't want a judge to think I'm slutty! Tom decides to temporarily move back to Kansas City, where he still has plenty of job connections from when he lived there previously. He can stay with friends for free and send every penny home to support us.

Even though we talk every day on the phone, I miss Tom terribly. I try hard to maintain the positive atmosphere for the kids that seems so effortless with him around. My recovering mind and body prove no match for the task. I am chronically exhausted, lonely, and stressed out.

After several weeks of being apart, I decide that we should be concerned not just with setting up our legal case for the best outcome, but also with doing what we can to please God so we can get His blessing on our union. My childhood programming swings into full effect as I reinstate the "no sex before marriage" boundary. Although Tom makes it clear that he disagrees with my premise, he is, not surprisingly, respectful of my wishes.

After a month, and while the kids are at Brad's, I am finally able to make the eleven-hour drive to see Tom. We meet up in a grocery store parking lot a couple of miles from where he is staying so I can follow him there and avoid getting lost. I can barely throw the van into park before I jump out the door and throw myself in his arms. We are seconds into an epic kiss when I start thinking that the back seat of the minivan looks pretty inviting. Not normally one for sex in public places, I am relieved to remember that I thought to put on pantyhose this morning. This sheer layer of nylon is the only thing keeping me honest. With great effort, I push Tom to arm's length and remind him of our rule. No sex until marriage. We want God to bless us, don't we? He reminds me that it is not his rule, and he also reassures me that he will honor *my* rule because he loves me.

Alone together again in his little basement bedroom later that night, we climb into bed. I am resolute, committed to the sanctity of marriage and redeeming the purity of our relationship. Tom wraps me up in his arms, and as I breathe in his sweet scent, I am overcome with passion. I freeze, frantically scanning my mind for any available source of willpower or resolve. Nothing. I want him! I *need* him! I don't know if I can do this. Why? I am at once confused, overwhelmed, shocked, and exquisitely aroused. The very core of who I know myself to be feels threatened. If there is one thing Anne-Lise is good at, it is controlling her sexual desires. I may be a failure at many other things, but this is my one forte.

Suddenly, a flash of inspiration crosses my mind. "Ask me to marry you!" I demand.

"I was getting to that," he splutters. "I have a ring picked out and…"

"Just ask me," I insist again.

"Okay," he concedes, with a hint of defeat in his voice. "Will you marry me?"

"YES!" I reply before he even finishes. "Now we can have sex."

My flimsy reasoning requires little explanation in the moment. We are both ready to connect. The next morning, Tom has some questions. I can't explain why I changed my mind, but I don't regret it. I tell him that we just need to hide it from the kids, so they don't grow up thinking it's okay to have sex before marriage. That will be easy while he's away. We will figure something out when he returns. I also assure him that once we are married, I will *never* tell him no. It's part of the deal he gets when marrying me!

Tom comes home to visit for the weekend about a month later. I make him go out to the couch early in the morning before the kids wake up, so it looks like he was there all night. I feel guilty, but I don't have a better idea. I need to connect with him. I need it. It feels good to desire sex and find it fulfilling. The nagging fear that I will later be punished by a vengeful God for breaking His rules is not enough to keep me from the sacred union I experience when Tom and I are together.

In late August, the kids are spending the last week of summer at Brad's. I'm back up in Kansas City visiting Tom when I get a call from the kids' school. Ella will be starting pre-school, Luke and Hannah are going into first and second grade respectively, and Gideon will be entering middle school. This is the only school the kids have ever attended, so I know the staff fairly well. The call is from the registrar, and I immediately worry that I've forgotten some necessary paperwork. No, she reassures me. She is just confused as to why I withdrew only two of my kids.

"There must be some mistake!" I insist. "I got everything in last week. We should be all good to go."

"No", comes the chilling reply. "Gideon and Hannah have been unenrolled."

I ask for more details, and she calls back fifteen minutes later to let me know they've been transferred to a school district thirty miles away. It's the district where Brad lives. My worst fear has been realized. He's taken the kids from me. I'm eleven hours away, with no legal recourse, terrified I will never see them again.

I call Brad in a panic, trying desperately to measure my tone and avoid exacerbating the situation. He and Karen have decided they will take the two older kids, and I will take the two younger ones. School has already started in their district, and Gideon and Hannah are doing well. I decide to hold my tongue for now. We confirm the pickup date and time when I will get Luke and Ella back, and I hang up the phone, crumpling to the ground like a discarded tissue.

Tom calls Brad back and has a private conversation during which he says something that prompts Brad to agree to return Hannah. Gideon will stay with him, he insists. Two days later, I pick up my three youngest children. Gideon has not come along to the drop-off, so I don't even get to see him. I begin setting appointments with lawyers first thing in the morning.

And that, dear reader, is the journey of a thousand steps that answers the question our lawyer from chapter one asked: "How did you get here?"

****

If this plot twist of a chapter has you reeling with uncertainty about how things are going to turn out, and especially if you are worried about whether I'm going to be able to adapt to this new, more supportive relationship, I encourage you to consider that there is probably a good reason this story caught your attention. If you'd like to discover what parts of your own story are most resonant and what gifts of healing they are ready to provide, please download the Study Guide for Chapter 8 at theuntherapist.com/chapter8.

PART TWO

The Becoming

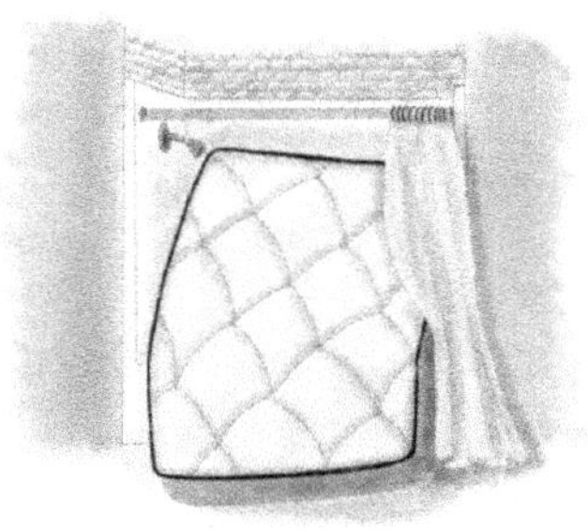

Chapter 9

Who Am I?

Chapter Framework:

-Old belief (before Untherapy): Who I am is wrong and broken. Because of this fact, I must work extra hard to cover my faults and appear normal to the outside world. Depression and anxiety are normal mental states and help me stay in line. I must live up to a higher standard than everyone else. I am excellent at loving and accepting others, but I require nothing in return. I need nothing beyond the knowledge that I am benefiting those who need me.

-The Untherapy Perspective: Existence is evidence of worthiness. The fact that we are alive in this time and space is proof that we deserve to be here. We can choose to accept that who we truly are (thoughts, feelings, and desires) is who we were meant to be. By accepting ourselves, we align with our Divine purpose and move toward the natural flow of life, which always seeks to support and encourage our growth and healing. Our unique combination of thought model, feeling type, life experiences, and true desires is perfectly optimized to support our best life. Our best efforts are always enough. Who we are is always enough. We are wired for connection. The more we understand about ourselves and others, the easier and more fulfilling all our relationships become. Life is a flow of giving and receiving. We are only as good at giving as we are at receiving.

"I define shame as the intensely painful feeling or experience of believing that we are flawed and therefore unworthy of love and belonging – something we've experienced, done, or failed to do makes us unworthy of connection." – Brené Brown

I meet with nine more lawyers after Mr. Lech before I find the one I trust will be able to restore my son to me. Greta is a pit bull of a divorce attorney who specializes in representing victims of domestic violence. I meet her through the abused women's shelter, where I have begun taking advantage of the free group and individual therapy sessions for which I am eligible. It is during a group session that I first hear the words, "You have the right to be safe in your own home." To be sure I understand, I raise my hand and ask, "So it's really *not* true that every wife secretly gets beaten?"

Some of the other women have filed criminal charges against their partners. I am thankful that the authorities here trust my word and understand why I never reported Brad. Talk therapy is a slow process where I often feel small and stupid, but the role-playing exercises are helping me find my voice, and I'm slowly learning how to set boundaries. Because I am a client of the shelter, Greta charges me a special rate that is a fraction of her normal fee.

A few days later, as we are working to draft the petition for sole custody that will require Brad to return Gideon, a sheriff shows up at my door to serve me divorce papers from Brad. I am both shocked and relieved. Now that Brad has initiated, I am off the hook with God. I didn't divorce him, so I am not culpable in God's eyes…I hope. Thankfully, Brad has not included any specific information on custody, so we still have full rights to ask the judge for whatever we want. It takes another six weeks and two hearings to get our ruling, but by mid-October, I accompany a local deputy to Gideon's new school and bring him home. He is happy to see his siblings again, but I feel strange around him, not sure if I've done the right thing bringing him back. I can't ask him specifically, but I know he has been brainwashed against me (and even more so, Tom) while he was gone.

Greta's hard work and determination to protect me and my kids teaches me so much about my worth as a human being and my ability as a mother. She also reassures me that it's perfectly safe for Tom to return to our home. The judge will not look unfavorably on his presence in my life, and it will not negatively affect the outcome of our case. He moves back in February of 2006, after being in Kansas City for a whole year. Having him back in the house takes an enormous amount of pressure off me. Our peaceful, stable environment is once again effortless. I still feel guilty for having sex before marriage, so I hold out as often as I can. Tom never pushes the issue. I still insist on the early morning couch pretense to keep up appearances. Whenever I forgo sex, I always reassure him that as soon as we are married, I will never again refuse him.

Ella falls into the habit of rising early and cuddling with him as they wake up together. She has taken to him effortlessly. The other kids are torn. Gideon is tight-lipped, but Luke and Hannah tell me about all the bad things Brad says about Tom. Tom has been very clear with me that we must never defend ourselves or say anything in retribution. Greta agrees that this is an important boundary to maintain for the kids' sake. It is important to let the kids come to their own realizations.

"The truth will always come out," Tom insists. I spend a lot of time biting my tongue in the moment and crying on his shoulder later.

Gideon resists Tom's parenting, reminding him, "You're not my dad."

Tom gently responds, "I know, Gideon. But I will always treat you like my own son. You can do whatever you want with that."

It takes until May to finalize the divorce. Karen throws up roadblocks at every turn, later admitting she just wanted to make Tom's life miserable because she knew how much he cared about the kids. Apparently, the ease with which Tom moved on after their divorce was insulting to her diva mentality, so she wanted to hit him where it hurt. I am granted sole custody, and Brad gets visitation every other weekend.

Greta makes sure to include a permanent injunction protecting me from ever having to speak to Brad again. She also asks the judge to waive the waiting period for remarriage, since the whole process has taken the better part of two years. He grants the request, and mid-morning on May 12, 2006, I pick up the kids from school without prior notice to attend a simple justice of the peace ceremony. We couldn't let them know ahead of time for fear they would mention it to Brad and he would try to sabotage our plans.

Now that we are married, Tom can wake up in bed with me every morning. I channel my Total Woman training from thirteen years before when I was entering my first marriage. I wait on Tom, quite literally, hand and foot. In my mind, it is time to pay back all the goodness he has showered on me. I busy myself being the uber wife I imagine his heart most desires. This makes him nervous, which is confusing for me. He is forever reminding me that he doesn't want me to do anything unless I *want* to do it. Oh, I definitely want to do all this. And more! So much more. When he does get upset or overwhelmed in the natural course of everyday life, I beat myself up, disappointed in my failure to be enough for him. Tom dislikes my self-deprecating behavior the most. I don't know how to stop it, but he cannot tolerate it. I learn to hide it better, but it still spills out when I'm under extreme pressure.

The kids start the new school year. Much to my delight, Tom attends their first parent/teacher conference with me (something Brad never did). Ella's kindergarten teacher declares that she has a "round bottom" and won't sit still. Ella is one of thirty five-year-olds being required to sit still for hours at a time and listen to a burned-out teacher who is one year from retirement. Luke is a second grader with debilitating anxiety. When he makes even a small mistake on his work, he disrupts class by crawling under a table and refusing to come out. Hannah, now in third grade, has been caught stealing personal items from her friend's backpack and is struggling in remedial reading class. Gideon is excelling in sixth grade, with advanced and honors classes, but he brings home three to four hours of homework every night, and his youthful spirit is being crushed under the stress of perfectionism.

That night, Tom brings up the idea of homeschooling. Hot tears of shame spring up unchecked. I have always wanted to homeschool, but when I brought it up to Brad when the kids were just starting off, he laughed scornfully at me for thinking I could teach them when I was so stupid and such a bad mom. Tom is sure I would do great. His most compelling argument, besides my abundance of intelligence, is the teacher/student ratio of one to four. Each of the kids is now one of thirty students in any given classroom. He argues that most of their problems would be resolved with more individualized attention. I know he's right, and I decide to trust his support and believe in my abilities.

We withdraw the kids over the Thanksgiving holiday. The transition is hell for the first two weeks. We realize the siblings have only been around each other in the foggy, rushed mornings before getting on the bus and at the end of the day when their energy is spent. Once we settle into the relaxed pace of a full night's sleep, leisurely morning starts, and no homework, they become a close-knit peer group. Ella gets her bounce back, Luke relaxes into the idea of imperfect learning, Hannah's reading starts to improve, and Gideon acclimates to a drastically reduced stress level. My prescriptions for antidepressants run out. I do not renew them.

The following March, we take a family road trip to Joplin, Missouri. Tom grew up here, and he wants me to meet the pastors of the church he grew up in. In his words, "They are the reason for everything good about me." When his parents divorced, they personally provided love and support that were critical to Tom's development. We spend a long weekend with them, eating scrumptious food around an enormous dining table, being warmly received by their little congregation of friendly faces, and touring the beautiful sights of the Ozark Mountains. I've lived in central Texas for most of my life, so seeing springtime bursting forth in an array of soft pinks, lacey whites, brilliant yellows, and deep greens is intoxicating. I fall in love with everything about this place. I want to live here.

Tom is hesitant to leave behind a thriving construction business, but he would do anything to make me happy, and he's an expert at fresh starts. The kids are flexible now that we homeschool, and the pastors just so happen to have a large renovation project underway on the old church building he knew so well when he was young. We are residents of Missouri in less than two months, staying with the pastors initially while Tom works full time on their church project. I take the kids to the local public library every day for lessons, and we picnic in a nearby park for lunch and playtime.

Brad sues me for custody, since the divorce decree prohibits me from moving more than one county away. At the hearing, Karen takes the stand with an incoherent string of accusations against Tom. "He's an irresponsible father and terrible provider. He has those kids sleeping on the floor in a church building."

After seven minutes, the judge cuts her off. "Tom is not on trial here," he explains, as he asks her to step down. For only the second time in his ten years on the bench, this judge in the most conservative district in Texas signs off on our out-of-state move. With the help of Gideon's testimony, Brad is ordered to take parenting and anger management classes and visit the kids in Joplin on his assigned weekends. He never once makes the trip to see them.

As spring gives way to summer and then summer to fall, the hundred-year-old towering oaks rustle majestically in the breeze above us. I revel in the novel beauty of the changing seasons. The kids make friends at church, and we participate in a local homeschool co-op for field trips, sports, and other learning opportunities. I redouble my efforts to be the perfect wife for Tom, adding new rules I'm picking up from my exposure to the nondenominational Christian belief system we are now a part of.

As I am adjusting to this new way of life, so opposite of anything I knew just a few short years ago, one night I bolt upright out of a disturbing dream. I glance at the bedside clock: 3:04 a.m. My ragged breathing wakes Tom, and through a sleepy haze, he reaches over. "You okay, babe?"

Still rattled by the terrifying images of the nonsensical nightmare, I struggle for words. "Did you know I was so messed up when you married me?"

He gathers me in his arms and gently kisses my forehead. "I knew you were struggling. I don't think of it that way. You're perfect. I love you no matter what. Go back to sleep."

I lie there the rest of the night, wrestling with the idea that I haven't earned this. Tears flow as I grapple with the realization that he has to navigate all my problems, and he deserves so much better. He knew I was a mess and loves me anyway. I can't wrap my head around it. Is this the "unconditional love" everyone keeps attributing to proper Jesus followers? It makes me feel awful. I could never love like this.

After five months of living with the pastors, their church building renovation project is complete, and we find a home in a neighboring town. Tom and I are soon asked to be the young adult pastors for the church, so we take on the spiritual care of a dozen members ages nineteen to twenty-nine. To give our small group of misfits a purpose and challenge, we begin a prayer ministry, which quickly catches the attention of the entire congregation.

Meanwhile, I have become obsessed with personality tests. Tom is forever finding new assessments that promise to illuminate various aspects of one's psyche, and he loves taking them and sharing them with me. I find this practice wholly frustrating. Whereas he eagerly consumes the results, applying what fits and casually dismissing what isn't helpful, I get stuck every time. Over and over, regardless of which theories we research, I find myself stuffed into a box that doesn't properly fit, mislabeled and misunderstood. What seems to be a fun little game for Tom has become for me a torturous reminder of how broken I am. Who even am I? It becomes abundantly clear that there is a fundamental difference between us: Tom knows, likes, and trusts himself. I cannot say the same for myself.

As I read through the results of the latest assessment, my heart strains to reconcile the labels it is handing me against a deeper truth buried just out of reach. This particular test result says I'm "The Helper". I'm supposed to be naturally gifted at serving and supporting. This is the third time I've taken this particular assessment in the past two months, and this is yet another different result. Tom agrees that I am a helper and seems unphased by the implications. I go blind with rage at the visual of myself chained to the kitchen sink, scrubbing dishes, while the rest of the family happily relaxes in an unreachable part of the house that is filled with comfort and happiness. I swallow hard, trembling with the effort to appear calm and reasonable. I am not okay, but I have no idea what to do about it.

After many such fiascos, I stumble into the concept of a simple four bucket model based on the natural way we experience our feelings. As we share this model with everyone we know, it gradually simplifies, perfects, and evolves into a concept I call Forces of Nature. Each person fits into one of four categories—Wind, Fire, Ocean, or Mountain, based on their core feeling type. Your Force is the perfect fit for you, and it empowers you to achieve what you most desire in your life. The limitation of only four choices seems a bit too overly simplified, but it is flexible enough to allow room for me to breathe without having a meltdown. Tom loves being a Wind, with all the free-flowing, light, changeable energy it brings. That must be what gives him the ability to tolerate my crazy. I instantly pick up the Fire label, since I am a doer who is always creating productive change with heated intensity. Gideon is an Ocean, which opens my eyes for the first time to the inherent differences between us. His methodical, cyclical perfectionism finally makes sense. My connection with my firstborn improves exponentially as I begin taking time to listen and create space for him to verbally process the depths of his weighty emotions. I decide that the rest of the kids are Winds. Their playful, light energy lends additional fun and flow to the household.

Over the next two years, the synergistic energy Tom and I apply to every undertaking seems to capture the imagination of all we encounter. Our primary focus is still on ministry, and based largely on our concerted efforts, the congregation has more than doubled in size. Before long, rumors stir from the top that Tom is trying to take over the church. Repeatedly, Tom exposes the false accusations directly to the head pastor, who has evolved from the mentor of his childhood into a close friend. But this man proves to be no match for the pressures of the small family dynamic within the religious construct. He crumbles under the fears and demands of the rest of his family, and after months of waffling, he finally kicks Tom (and the rest of us) out of the church.

Before we were unceremoniously banned from this church, we had been busy determining everyone's Force of Nature, using it as a tool to help improve relationships and increase emotional intelligence. As we grapple with the betrayal, I can construct a narrative that explains what happened in terms of the natural feeling type of each key player. The head pastor was a Mountain, and as such, would do anything to maintain personal structural integrity. He internalized conflict and sought to maintain external peace at all costs. He was drawn to Tom's Windy, non-judgmental nature as a rare gift for one in a pastoral position. As Tom became a trusted friend and confidant, it created jealousy in the rest of his family. His wife was an Ocean, whose deep, cyclical, methodical processing resisted the change brought by Tom's lighthearted flow. Their son, who was in charge of the music and youth ministries, was a Fire. His temper flared as he tried to control the players in his future empire. His frustration at the perceived loss of power caused him to join forces with his mom and launch a smear campaign that resulted in our family being ousted.

The sudden shock of being cut off from all our spiritual and social connections in one fell swoop leaves a lasting wound. Tom experiences a deep crisis of faith that takes years to resolve. He eventually refers to it as "the best worst thing that needed to happen." He also decides, after having set aside alcohol for over two years, that tequila is going to be part of his life again. Despite the emotional carnage of this entire fiasco, I am comforted to know that each person who caused us pain was not doing it with evil intention. I clearly see how they were acting from a place of fear and personal triggers that devolved into a perfect storm based on their own lack of self-awareness and emotional intelligence. I become convinced that understanding human behavior and teaching emotional literacy is my one true calling.

I'm finally ready to introduce Tom to my parents. We visit Mom and Dad and all my siblings back in Texas for Thanksgiving. It has taken over three years for me to be ready to deal with my shame and the potential backlash I might face from all the hurt I caused them when I went back to Brad. I'm also nervous because Tom isn't part of the religion we grew up in. Even though I haven't been a part of that belief system for years now, I am afraid Dad is going to reject Tom because he isn't one of the chosen ones.

At a post-meal bonfire, Tom drinks homemade wine with Mom and puts his arm around my not-so-cuddly father. As I sit chatting with one of my sisters, I hear Tom's voice booming from the other side of the idyllic holiday scene. "I love your daughter with all my heart. I promise I will always protect her and care for her. She is the most incredible and special woman in the world." I smile self-consciously with secret delight. Dad does not have anything bad to say about Tom.

As I continue to homeschool the kids, now ages ten, twelve, fourteen, and sixteen, I start helping Tom paint on the weekends. One particularly warm Sunday afternoon in May, we run out of paint on a job in a neighboring town. Tom has been painting for thirty years by this point. He *never* runs out of paint. Begrudgingly, and because the paint store closest to the job is located on the other side of town, I call in the order ahead of time. As luck would have it, I've called the wrong location, and we end up trekking all the way back to the store nearest our house.

As we are paying, the tornado siren, located just two blocks away, drowns our attempts at lighthearted small talk. Since it's on the way back to the job, Tom and I swing by the house for a quick check on the kids before we head back to finish painting. As we pull up in front of the house, the kids are milling about on the front porch, looking up at the strange green clouds swirling overhead. The tornado siren blares a second warning. Tom leaps out of the truck and sprints to the porch, yelling, "Get inside! Get inside!" He orders us into the middle bathroom. We pile into the bathtub, Ella climbing onto my lap and the rest of the kids holding on to each other. Tom drags a mattress from the bedroom and leans it over the top of us with the weight of his body.

Within seconds, the tornado bears down on us. Tom's booming voice reaches through the mattresses as he prays out loud for safety and mercy. I instinctively repeat his words, rhythmically chanting, "Jesus, save us. Jesus, save us." The kids are crying and chanting along with us. The roar of a hundred freight trains overwhelms my senses as power lines explode with sizzling cracks coupled with impressive sprays of fireworks. The percussive shatter of glass punctuates the mayhem like an infinite torrent of crashing cymbals. So. Much. Glass. The house trembles, and even though Tom has us covered by the mattress, I feel Ella's body being sucked up out of my arms. I grip her more tightly, determined that if the storm takes her, it will have to take me, too. My eardrums throb with excruciating pressure, and seconds later, the whole middle part of the roof breaks free and blows away. A strange green pallor streams in from the gaping hole above, and as suddenly as it began, all is silent.

We are silent, too. Tom removes the mattress. We are all in shock. Gideon tells us he saw a massive angel stretching its wings over us in protection the whole time. The little ones sob. I check them for scratches or bruises. Nothing. The bathroom window is the only one still intact. We pick our way through what is left of the rest of the house, a blender of broken furniture, twisted fabric, and shattered glass. At length, we manage to dig out shoes for everyone. As we open the front door and look out over our neighborhood, we are greeted by a sharp hissing sound and the smell of natural gas. A mixture of insulation, twigs, dirt, and other debris covers everything. Naked trees, stripped of all their greenery, flap their few remaining broken branches in the heavy air. And this is our view, as far as the eye can see. The Joplin Tornado of 2011 was an EF-5 that still stands as the seventh deadliest and number one most costly in recorded history.

I have been teaching Forces of Nature for over a year now, and one thing I know is that Fires feel the best when they are excelling under pressure. This is my chance to shine. As Tom begins planning where we can take shelter for the night, he instructs me to pack up our valuables. I go back in the house and decide to start with the computer. I can't. Shock and overwhelm collapse my body to the floor, where I heave myself into the filth and rubble. There is no Fire left in me. I don't know who I am.

Even though our insurance company can put us up at a hotel, there is none available with running water, so we decide to stay at our office on Main Street, a few blocks from the disaster zone. For six months, we live in that storefront, sleeping on the floor and eating out of an electric skillet. We rig a shower by attaching a garden hose with a spray attachment to the bathroom sink, and we pile our clothes on plastic tables in place of closets. At Tom's prompting, to help reduce the pressure on me, we enroll the kids in an online homeschool program that includes teaching and tutoring. Nothing about this crisis has brought out even a shred of the productive problem-solving I thought to be my nature.

I finally come to terms with the fact that I am not a Fire. I try on Ocean and even Mountain for size. I'm not methodical or patient enough to be an Ocean, and I'm way too extroverted and excitable to be a Mountain. The inevitable realization creeps over me like a death sentence. I am a Wind. Tom reminds me that discovering more truth about myself should set me free, not bog me down. It just feels so…dangerous. It is not safe to be a Wind—they are too…silly. I consider my husband and my kids, my friends and other acquaintances. I know a lot of Winds, and I love them all. Why couldn't I be one, too?

Then I realize something. My dad is a Mountain. He likes to feel fixed and stable. He craves internal focus and quiet space for introspection. If I am a Wind, I probably drove him crazy with all my wild, open-hearted lack of predictability growing up. "Don't be silly"—his old admonition haunts me like a bad dream, only now I finally understand why. Maybe it is safe to be a Wind. Maybe he just didn't know how to handle it. I realize my mom is also a Wind. My frustration at her character becomes clear as day. She naturally wants to flow, light and free. She chooses to subordinate her nature to her husband to fit the dynamic they have established. It's what I tried to do all those years as a child, and then even more completely in my marriage to Brad. Oh, and Brad must be an Ocean. The depth of his processing kept me in a continual state of drowning. I never let myself come up for air, and I never used my true lighthearted, non-judgmental, Windy nature for the benefit of the relationship. As I allow myself to play with the idea of choosing light, flexible, easy, flowing options for my life, it's like I am waking out of a thirty-seven-year sleep. Maybe life doesn't have to be so hard. Maybe I can enjoy my natural Windy way of feeling, and maybe someday I can even learn to like who I naturally am.

****

If you've ever struggled with shame (a sense of being bad or wrong because of who you inherently are), the Chapter 9 Study Guide was made for you. Having a simple and concrete way to understand your natural characteristics and release self-judgment can change everything. Download it now at theuntherapist.com/chapter9.

Chapter 10

Things Come Up to Come Out

Chapter Framework:

-Old belief (before Untherapy): I will never be as good as other people. Some people are just better than others, and I am always on the losing end of that comparison. It is important to try to repay others for their kindness and love to me, especially if they gave it freely before I understood its value.

-The Untherapy Perspective: Things come up to come out. Traumatic experiences provide the precise healing opportunities we are most ready for. When something bothers us, it is presenting the ideal next opportunity to heal and grow. As we process these triggers, we make space for our natural upward evolution with the right pace and timing that works with and expands our capacity to thrive. Everyone is doing their best with what they have from where they are. Even (and especially) when we cannot understand why, we can choose to acknowledge that each person got to this moment the same way we did: by trying to figure it out the best way they knew how.

"You are not meant to bear that which you find unpleasant; you are meant to change it." –Mike Dooley

After six months of living at the office, we move to a spacious home outside of town. We are all still processing the trauma of the tornado. Ella panics at the sight of a single fluffy cloud in the sky and decides we need to move somewhere that doesn't have any weather at all. We are transitioning from homeschooling to the less structured tenants of unschooling, and we give her full latitude to immerse herself in the study of meteorology. To this day, she can interpret a radar map at a single glance and accurately predict tomorrow's weather with an evaluation of the sky at sunset.

Tom beats himself up about not being more careful when he was protecting us during the tornado. What if that window had shattered inward like all the others did? He would've been a human pin cushion. It would've taken months to recover. He should have thought it through and protected himself better! I notice a pattern in myself that bothers me. Every time he gets vulnerable with me, opening up about a doubt or fear, I become uncomfortable and resistant. Even though I know it's not fair, I kind of need him to be invincible all the time. When he falters, my foundation feels shaky and uncertain. It's hard to reconcile that my knight in shining armor is also a human with needs of his own.

I challenge myself to practice open-hearted Windy support of his Wind feelings, which theoretically should be an effortless match. When he is processing something that is hard for him, I practice saying, "You are allowed to feel whatever you feel. It's okay for you to not be okay." I don't know if I really mean it, but I say it anyway. I *want* to mean it. I work hard to resist the urge to fix him and dismiss his struggles. These are things I am secretly practicing on myself, and it helps me to extend the same grace to Tom. I begin to feel less estranged from my own personality and more capable of holding space for his healing. Over time, I find that I can return the gift of non-judgmental presence that Tom has been blessing me with since the moment we met.

The experience of the tornado has revealed another problem. Tom plays out a scenario where I die, and he asks the chilling question, "What would happen to the kids?" After we moved to Joplin, they continued to see Brad and Karen at least once a year for a week-long vacation, but they have since divorced. Brad hasn't made any attempt to see them since he and Karen broke up, and the thought of the kids being under his care at this point goads me into decisive action.

We decide Tom needs to legally adopt the kids. They are now eleven, thirteen, fifteen, and seventeen. In the state of Missouri, a child over the age of fifteen must also consent to the adoption. Hannah eagerly signs off. Ella asks if she can sign a paper, too. Luke expresses his excitement with his typical understated shyness. The guardian ad litem interviews each of the kids and does a home inspection. He also interviews friends and family. My mom calls after her phone interview to report that she told the attorney that she and Dad "wish our daughter had married Tom in the first place."

Gideon wrestles with the decision. Gradually over the years, he has come to respect and love Tom as a father figure. He has been learning the drywall trade for years now, and Tom is setting him up for a lucrative future in construction. But Gideon was Brad's favorite and the only one who had some genuine good memories with him. There is a loyalty that would be severed, and Gideon doesn't take it lightly. The guardian ad litem informs him that since he is only a month from turning eighteen, it might be easier to just keep things as they are.

After more careful thought, during which Tom and I do our best to honor his Ocean need to process fully and deeply, Gideon finally opts in favor of adoption so he can share the same last name as his siblings and be in a better position to take custody of them if anything ever happened to both Tom and me. All those early years of caring for his younger siblings continue to influence his priorities. Brad does not respond to multiple attempts to be reached by phone, email, and postal service, so our adoption attorney takes out an ad in the newspaper local to his last known address.

On April 12, 2012, our entire family officially shares the same last name. Tom's oldest son is no longer their stepbrother, but now their half-brother: same dad, different mom. Tom jokes that he "ordered" all his kids *after* they were potty trained! Since he's already been their acting father for eight years, there is no change in the household other than the outward, legal expression of what already existed in principle. When the new birth certificates come in the mail, Ella asks for a copy. She colors and decorates it with stickers, storing it in a special spot near her bed.

Meanwhile, with encouragement from my good friend Amber, who has the requisite professional connections, I go pro with my emerging personality model. I begin training in corporate manufacturing settings, starting with management and moving on to team leads and line workers, the vast majority of whom are men. Tom attends sessions as an observer in the back of the room, and his observations and insight prove invaluable as I develop more comprehensive components. In the men's bathroom during breaks, he overhears them complain about the "stupid training" they have been forced to attend when they would just rather be doing their job. I hate the idea of teaching people who were paid by someone else to learn, but it's a great training ground for me to hone my skills and program. I also love making money at the one thing I feel like I was born to do.

A referral leads to a connection at a local university, where I teach for three years as a guest lecturer. We also use my system to train the employees in Tom's construction business, educating them on how to better understand their coworkers, increase communication, and even take the knowledge home to improve their family relationships. On my free weekends, I teach local workshops in the same office where we lived after the tornado. Tom and I work with couples and families, and I start doing individual one-on-one sessions, both in person and online.

These individual sessions reveal the significance of trauma in the development of personality. I dig into the study of neuroscience, discovering the concept of neuroplasticity and learning how neurons can be reprogrammed to fire in new, more supportive ways. I learn that most of the foundational programs we carry with us our entire lives are formed by the time we are five years old. Without conscious reprogramming, we live our whole lives on auto-pilot, acting out what felt normal to us when we were small children.

I discover Faster EFT, which is a modification of the original emotional freedom technique I resisted as "voodoo" years earlier during my religious phase. Sessions from multiple practitioners give me the experience of instant healing as I learn the power of releasing my past trauma and programming with gentle finger taps to various acupressure points on my face and chest. This healing shows up in life-altering ways as my capacity to hold space for the emotions of myself and others increases. My hair-trigger sensitivity to any perceived criticism steadily morphs into a calmer self-awareness that allows me to listen and really understand what others are trying to communicate. Beyond the practitioner-led sessions, I learn how to perform these simple tapping techniques on myself in the moment. I develop the ability to create space between the trigger and the response, reclaiming a sense of Divine peace that feels downright luxurious. I teach this skill to everyone I know.

For the first time in my life, I am able recall painful experiences without spiraling into depression or panic. I can look back at my marriage to Brad and see how I played into his sexual addiction and mental illness, exacerbating his worst symptoms by supporting his every whim in the name of godly submission. I see how I used the lie of female powerlessness to practice a "holy" learned helplessness. I could place all the decision-making responsibility on him and never have to step into the deeper, scarier parts of my own vulnerability. All I had to do was follow him to the letter of the law, and I believed I was off the hook. No, I didn't get to make any of my own decisions, but I also didn't have to take any risks.

I can imagine Brad as a small child, a victim of chronic sexual and emotional abuse, who learned to survive by manipulating anyone who would let him. I forgive him for hurting me and, more importantly, forgive myself for not knowing better. I release the years of shame I've been fostering for the damage I caused my kids. As they navigate their teen years, I am humbled and privileged that they allow me to help them release their own layers of abuse, neglect, and pain that formed their earliest programming.

As Luke heals from the wound of rejection he incurred before birth when I had planned on giving him up for adoption to Celeste, his adult personality begins to emerge, and I realize I have mistaken his feeling type for Wind all these years. His Mountain feelings have struggled to maintain space in our predominantly Wind household, rife with competitive talking and spur-of-the-moment plan changes. I tap out my mom-guilt and gratefully embrace my new interpretation of his calm, reticent nature. I also encourage him to go to his room more frequently and enjoy his own peace and quiet, rather than constantly expecting him to participate in the hubbub of our family dynamic. Our relationship improves exponentially.

I go back further and work on my relationship with my parents. I let go of the need for my dad to be something other than a Mountain or to be more accepting of my Windy nature. I forgive my mom for not teaching me how to use my voice and set boundaries for myself. And I forgive them both for not teaching me that life is for living: that it is an exercise in trusting Divine guidance to spur us into pursuing what we most desire in a grand adventure of self-discovery and evolution. They came up in a different era, with their own difficult childhood programming, where reality was much harsher. Of course, they wouldn't have been able to teach me something they themselves didn't know.

As I wrestle with the blame and shame of my childhood, I only see my parents about once a year. My newly found freedom and forgiveness do not increase the frequency of my visits, but they most certainly improve the quality. I still find it hard to be in their environment of curated behavior and religious restrictions, but it feels like the ultimate freedom to know that they have always loved me with all their hearts, simply because I exist. Nothing I do could ever change that.

As I think back to my past, it plays like an old movie that doesn't carry any of its previous power. I can watch it if I want, but it's not nearly as compelling as going out and enjoying my real life as it is happening right now. I understand Tom's stability as a direct result of his deep connection with his own father. His dad was a Wind, just like him, and Tom was a change-of-life baby, born when Pops was already in his forties. Tom got the benefit of a mature father who intuitively knew how to nurture his son with non-judgmental acceptance in an environment of straight-forward freedom. This created a solid foundation that helped Tom navigate the later years after his parents divorced without losing his own identity.

I finally release the last vestiges of guilt over living with and having sex with Tom prior to getting legally married. I clearly see that the sacred commitment we made to each other in our first week together was more than sufficient to bond our union on a Divine plane. We decide that our official anniversary celebration date will honor our first night together as a couple, rather than the date we were finally able to make the marriage official in the eyes of the law. I shed a lifetime of shame like a worn garment that has lost its usefulness forever.

I vow to teach my children the value of consent, Divine guidance, and personal intuition above external rules and religious guidelines taught by other people. I spend numerous guided visualization sessions sending love and support back to my younger self. I view her with compassion and empathy, knowing she did the very best she knew to do in the moment. I also understand that none of that striving gained her a single iota of worth or value. I relax into the idea that I don't have to read the Bible to know God, and I stop thinking of the Divine as a bearded, angry white man on a throne in the sky.

The more clients I work with, the more I understand the universal nature of trauma programming. Whether passively or actively accumulated, these programs affect our ability to interact with reality in the present. To varying degrees, we are all zombies, mindlessly walking our predetermined patterns we've been practicing our whole lives. As I proactively slough off these layers of old habits, my life blossoms naturally into an exciting adventure full of possibilities and promise.

For our ten-year anniversary, in the fall of 2014, Tom and I celebrate for a week at an exclusive resort in the Dominican Republic. On our last evening, we go for one more dip in the crystal-blue ocean. There's a red flag warning signaling the danger of a rip current, so we decide to just wade in up to our knees and call it good. Without warning, an enormous swell of water pulls us under. Instantly, we are another hundred yards from shore. I've read the signs at the beach entrance that tell you what you're supposed to do if you are caught in the rip current, but I am in shock and have no recollection of what to do. I'm not a strong swimmer, and the water is well over my head. Just as I break the water's surface, another ten-foot wave breaks mercilessly overhead, and under I go. Tom is twenty feet to my left and calling out instructions: "Relax, breathe, wave is coming, let it wash over you…" And under I go again. I've swallowed massive amounts of ocean water, and I choke it up as I gasp for another breath. I am angry at the waves. I just need a tiny break to catch my breath. Their relentless blows push me under just before I can fill my lungs.

Tom is yelling again, his panicked voice rising above the crashing waves. "Save my wife! Save my wife!" His cries are directed at a group of lifeguards who are already plunging through the waves toward us. They all seem to be coming my way, and in my panicked state, I fear they will leave Tom to die.

"Save my husband too!" I try to scream, but the sound is swallowed by the waves. Under I go again. When I come back up, they are tossing me a flotation buoy. They turn and begin heading back to shore. I see a rope floating behind them and lunge forward to grab it. I need them to help pull me in! I temporarily lose track of Tom as I work against the relentless current to make my way to shore. Of course, the buoy was also attached to the rope, but I don't discover that until I feel sand beneath my feet. The three lifeguards who pulled me in are bent over, catching their breath after the herculean effort.

A fourth lifeguard is helping Tom in. We collapse on our backs in the sand, chests heaving in utter exhaustion. I bore four children at home without drugs, and that was a walk in the park compared to almost drowning. A safety supervisor appears and encourages us to go to the hospital. I apologize profusely for the trouble I've already caused. I am confident that I am physically fine, but I'm terribly ashamed for causing these brave men such a hard day's work. Tom is talking to the supervisor. We are the twenty-third and twenty-fourth rescues of the year. Only one did not make it, because he was a belligerent drunk who refused help.

In a flash of inspiration, I decide that we should get a photo. If we can pose for a picture, they will be assured that we are okay and don't need medical assistance. I gather the lifeguards around us and flash a broad smile while Tom's eyes gaze blankly off into the distance. It is the ultimate awkward family photo.

Back in the room, Tom and I pass out on the bed, fully clothed, our legs hanging off the edge down to the floor. The haunting refrain "save my wife" rings in my dreams. It takes weeks to work up the courage to ask, "Would you have died out there for me?" He explains that he knew how to swim to safety, but he didn't want to leave me, and yes, he would die for me if he needed to. No question. I remember how quickly I forgot his whereabouts as soon as the buoy was in my hands. Am I a bad person? Sometimes being married to such an amazing human makes me feel small and inept. There is no way to express this self-deprecating sentiment to Tom. He's even more allergic to my self-flagellation now than in our early days. We are both Winds. I've worked through loads of my trauma. Why do we still think of things so differently?

****

If you've ever felt stuck in your old patterns or thwarted by years of bad habits, the Study Guide for Chapter 10 was made for you. Download it at theuntherapist.com/chapter10 to discover a whole new way to overcome limiting beliefs and naturally evolve into the best version of yourself you never thought you'd be able to achieve.

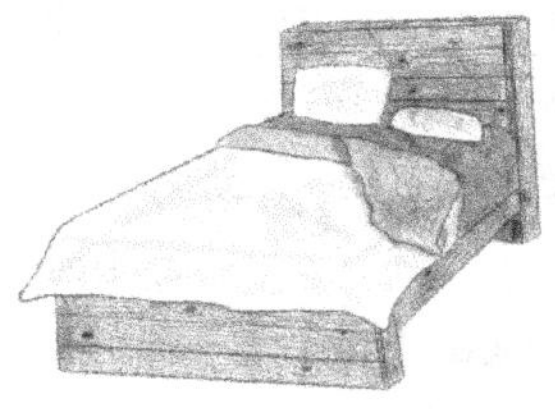

Chapter 11

Dare to Desire

Chapter Framework:

-Old belief (before Untherapy): I am required to have certain people and circumstances in my life. It is my job to make sure nothing bad happens to these essential components of my life. I cannot survive without external validation. I owe an unending debt of gratitude to those who have chosen to be in relationship with me, and I must subvert my desires in order to repay my debt. I am not allowed to have what I most desire until everyone around me has what they want. My desires are less important. There are only two options: my own happiness or the happiness of those I love. Processing difficult emotions and releasing trauma must be torturous and dramatic. Fear is the most effective way to keep myself obedient to what is right.

-The Untherapy Perspective: Fear is a tool that faithfully brings to our awareness the next thing we are ready to release. Because we are wired for healing and growth, we can find gentle protocols that allow us to release trauma and reprogram our own minds with ease and grace. We always have more options than we realize. We are each responsible for our own boundaries and for the effective communication of those boundaries. We do not owe anything to anyone other than to take 100 percent responsibility for our own thoughts, feelings, and desires. Even when we are failing miserably, we cannot help but continue to learn and mature.

"These dreams ain't all that they seem. I know that they could hurt me, so won't you hold my hand if they come true." –Maddie Poppe

As I continue to train and teach, my model of human behavior takes shape. I start calling my system "Untherapy" and myself the Untherapist. I am not anti-therapy, but I have personally experienced the limitations of conventional talk therapy. I know all too well that our conscious growth is limited by our subconscious programming. Without shedding the requisite layers of contradictory information, we can talk around the same mountain to infinity and never take a single step forward. I am working on a model that will help people determine when they need outside help and what modality and practitioner will work best for them. In addition, I am creating a way for clients to help themselves in those critical trigger moments when they need it most, which is rarely at a scheduled appointment.

I am still looking for an explanation that addresses how two people with the same feeling type, such as Tom and me (both Winds), can have such a fundamentally different approach to life. Then I discover Gretchen Rubin's The Four Tendencies. She developed this construct to explain the different ways people handle expectations. As I work with clients using her categories, I adapt her framework to my own Untherapy system. I begin to use her Four Tendencies to explain the different models we naturally use to organize our thoughts. I've finally found the missing piece of my human behavior puzzle. From my work with trauma and programming, I already know that we create the reality of our lives from a place of conscious thought, located in our prefrontal cortex, which I call our "Creative Genius". Now I know why two people with the same feeling type can go about doing this in such different ways. It is because they *think* in completely different ways.

Each of us has one of four possible thought models, which we use to automatically select, organize, and prioritize our conscious thoughts. We have only one type, and it is optimized from birth to give us the best way of thinking for our unique needs and desires. The four types are Rebel, Upholder, Questioner, and Obliger. Rebels organize their thoughts like clouds in an infinite sky, which is to say, they don't really "organize" them at all. They pick and choose, grab and go, with whatever thought cloud catches their fancy in the moment. Sometimes they let go of an existing cloud, even if it's working great, just to explore other options. And if they see you removing one of their clouds from their field of potentiality, that is *definitely* the very cloud they were about to select. Tom's mysterious mind is finally revealed. As a Rebel, it's not that he has a rebellious nature per se, but more so that he defies control and restriction in all its forms, for himself and for others. He wants unlimited access to his thought clouds without the inhibiting force of external (or internal) rules and regulations. His Wind energy complements this free flow of ideas beautifully, creating the quintessential "young at heart" and "in the moment" mentality that endures despite his age and life experience.

Upholders are the opposite. Their thoughts are organized like boxes. They are the collectors of rules and regulations, using whichever ones will lend structure to their personally prioritized, orderly rows and stacks of rigid, structured thought. My dad is an Upholder. His seemingly inexhaustible ability to hold a course and abide by a set of internally chosen directives finally has an explanation. Coupled with his Mountain feeling type, Dad is the perfect model of "set in stone". I now understand his ability to faithfully keep a personal journal practice for his entire adult life without ever skipping a day. His exercise regimen, the nightly Bible studies, and his chosen profession of research scientist all align with his unique combination of feeling type and thought model to create a man who religiously upholds the principles and parameters that make sense to him.

Conversely, Questioners organize their thoughts like solving a puzzle. Their infinite capacity to ask questions and seek answers lends itself to thorough research which, if overplayed, quickly devolves into obsessive rumination and analysis paralysis. When faced with a personally compelling issue, they instinctively search for all the necessary pieces to the puzzle and put them together in a way that seems to naturally click and provide the clarity and resolution they innately seek. Gideon and Ella are both Questioners. They share an aptitude for research and a compulsion for problem solving, but Gideon's Ocean feeling type creates a more methodical and cyclical result, whereas Ella's Wind feeling type lends a lighter flow and less intensity to her process.

Finally, Obligers organize their thoughts to achieve a five-star review. Their minds are optimized to consider how their actions affect the end result for others. They inherently seek to produce the most favorable outcome for the particular situation at hand. As with the other thought models, they are creating an internal reference point, so it must be more than just the feedback offered by external sources. They want to *feel* like they've created a five-star experience. My mom is an Obliger. This explains her seemingly infinite capacity to serve and give of herself without acting on her own needs or desires. Coupled with her Wind feeling type, this way of thinking helps her automatically prioritize the preferences of others before her own. I select Obliger as my own thought model. I am a lot like my mom, and I feel like this model is the most accurate in describing my innate drive to serve, accommodate, and please others (especially Tom).

My Untherapy model of human behavior is complete. I have renamed my one-on-one sessions "Superlearnings" and reduced their duration from two hours down to one. The results from this simplified approach are more profound and lasting than any previous efforts. One of Tom's long-time employees is able to overcome a drug addiction he has battled his whole life. A couple on the brink of divorce is able to fully reconcile after the husband releases his codependency. A client who was raped as a teen stops having night terrors and repairs her relationship with her husband. I have hundreds of stories like this. I imagine the transformation Brad could've experienced if he'd had access to this kind of help.

As the kids grow up and move out, I see an opportunity to make a full-time career out of my Untherapy practice. I still help Tom in the drywall and paint contracting business, and I enjoy the paperwork and bookkeeping side of things, but the daily grind of slinging paint has completely lost its appeal. I am eager to move on to the next chapter of my life.

Tom runs his business like a good Wind Rebel. His excellent navigation skills and penchant for what I call "people-building" have grown into a thriving business with an average of twenty loyal, hard-working employees at any given time. Gideon stays in the construction industry but takes his skills to another company with more structure that proves a better fit for his Ocean Questioner personality. For the time being, Hannah and Luke continue to work in the family business, which provides them a steady source of income until they land on something that aligns with a deeper passion. Ella, who is the only kid still living at home, partners with Tom and starts running the paint phase of new construction by herself shortly before she turns nineteen.

Our biggest challenge is finding good employees who want to learn the trade. Years of social pressure to get a college degree over learning a trade have resulted in a massive deficit in the labor pool. As I continue to work full time, my patience wears thin. I've cut back on Superlearning sessions and no longer have time for weekend workshops. I begin to criticize Tom's decisions and management of the company. I feel trapped and stymied. He insists that it is holistic: we are in all of this together, and if we try to separate it, everything will suffer. I am part of the construction business. He is part of Untherapy. It's all a matter of pace and timing, he assures me. But I'm sick of doing a job I don't like when the career I want is dangling just past the end of my fingertips. Am I going to have to wait until everyone else gets what they want before I can have what I want? I don't say it out loud, but I realize with an old familiar sinking heart that maybe I'm just supposed to help everyone else. Maybe there's not enough left over at the end for me to get what I really want.

On a sunny morning in early October of 2019, I am driving to a remodel job in a town about an hour away. As usual, I'm on the phone with Tom, using the drive time to go over the schedule and strategy for the next couple of days' worth of work. He lets me know about an extra project that needs to be squeezed in before I start the next big house. In that instant, something deep inside me snaps. I feel the color drain out of my face. My vision narrows, and I grip the wheel tightly with both hands, straining to stay between the lines on the highway. Before I realize what I'm saying, I've begun a full-blown diatribe against Tom and this business. Years of serving and waiting, helping and assisting, delaying my own desires in favor of others, spur me on like a million screaming demons. The other end of the phone goes silent while Tom lets me finish. We talk about it here and there over the next few days with no progress. He can't understand what has happened, and I can't make myself care.

Over the coming weeks, I remain in a state of almost constant trigger, completely oblivious to how I am acting. I have somehow crossed an invisible threshold. None of the old ways I'm supposed to care about seem to work anymore. I am angry, but with no target. I blame Tom, but mostly out of convenience. Intuitively, I know this is not his fault, and yet I want it to be.

By Thanksgiving Day, we are at an impasse. I decide to go to work just to be away from everyone. I know there won't be any other crews on the jobsite, so it will give me some privacy to sort myself out. Tom calls in the late afternoon to check on me. We argue, and he suggests that I seek outside help. I hang up, utterly defeated. I've never felt like a bigger fraud in my life. I've come so far. I think back to the best days I ever had with Brad, and they were *still* far worse than even this present moment. Why can't I just suck it up and be grateful for what I *do* have?

In that moment, with Tom's suggestion to get outside help still ringing in my head, I make the bravest decision of my life. It is Thanksgiving Day. There is not a single person I could call for help right now. I grab a pen and paper and head to the master bathroom, where the jacuzzi tub is masked off with plastic to protect it from paint. I climb in, take a deep breath, and get to work. After forty-five minutes of applying my Superlearning protocol to myself, I am spent.

Through eyes swollen with tears, I type up the following text and send it to Tom:

I just finished working on myself, and here are my takeaways:

I have space to heal

I have time to heal

I am healing

I am taking responsibility

It's okay to struggle

Live in the moment

It's not my fault

It's not anyone else's fault

Everything is exactly as it should be

The only way to make it better is to "be" better (as in, focus on being in the moment more)

Make peace with being at peace

I don't feel like any of those points explain how I got here, so I still feel like I need outside help, but at least I realize this is 100 percent in my mind and not the fault or responsibility of anyone else. I sent this hoping it would help you understand.

On its face, this text belies the depth of transformation that occurred during my bathtub Superlearning. I have just experienced a moment of spontaneous evolution. Things have been gradually changing over time, and now, suddenly, I have leapt forward into another dimension of awareness. Every epiphany scribbled through hot tears of desperation felt like another light bulb illuminating the dark recesses of my mind. I stepped into that tub as a suffering, codependent, helpless damsel in distress, searching for a savior to give her permission to live. I emerged as a warrior goddess with irrefutable proof that I could slay my own demons. This feeling is strange and ill-fitting, like stiff new leather shoes that have yet to be softened and formed with use.

Over the span between Thanksgiving and Christmas, I exist in a pseudo-fugue state. Tom has begun sleeping upstairs in the spare bedroom. He tells me it is too painful to share a bed with a stranger whom he knows so well and not at all. He is also genuinely worried that he will lash out in his sleep and hurt me. He has had active dreams his whole life, but when he gets especially disturbed, he has been known to land a good punch without ever waking up. He doesn't want to risk it. I am glad to have the space. For the first time in our relationship, I have no desire to be around him. There is a deep ache in my heart. I miss him, but I do not want him. I am so, so angry. For the first time in our relationship, I find myself asking the unthinkable: "Is he still the one?" I've built my life with this person. Our entire family, business, finances, friendships, and future are inextricably intertwined.

I squeeze in as many sessions with a tapping practitioner as the busy holiday schedule will allow. She uses a different method than my Superlearnings, but because I know exactly what I need, these sessions produce massive shifts for me.

As I release deeply embedded layers of old programming, I am emboldened to enumerate my grievances to Tom and demand change. It feels like we are no longer a match, and I cannot imagine this is all my fault. He needs to be working on fixing all his problems just as hard as I am working on mine. I demand that he work with a practitioner as well. He submits intake forms, but before his first scheduled appointment can happen, I am in such a desperate state that he offers to let me take the session in his place. I jump at the chance.

I also have two friends, Amber and Julie, who know and love both Tom and me. I lean on their support to guide me through my most difficult moments. For the first time in my adult life, I call my mom to ask for advice. She is the one person I know who has never cracked under the pressure. I must know her secret.

"Do you ever get angry?" I ask.

"Oh sure," she replies. "Your dad just tells me to stop it and I do." She mails me a beautifully scripted Bible study that she's compiled especially for me so I can learn what God teaches about anger.

On Christmas Eve, Tom goes over to Amber's house for some support. She's a Mountain Rebel we have known for over ten years, and her wisdom and perspective always seem to help both of us. I collapse on the couch at home in utter exhaustion. My Spotify plays softly in the background, when a Maddie Poppe song called "Not Losing You" comes on. It's one of those transcendent moments where the artist reaches into your soul and breathes life into the feelings you couldn't access. As she sings the lines "These dreams ain't all that they seem / I know that they can hurt me / So won't you hold my hand if they come true," I break down sobbing. That's it! That's exactly how I feel right now. I know I want this new career, helping to transform people's lives on a grand scale, but I also know it will be different than my expectations. I want to do it *with* Tom. We got to this point together, and I want to continue doing life together, whatever that ends up looking like.

As soon as the song is over, I text the link to Tom. Four minutes later, Amber calls. She excitedly facilitates an exchange of good will between Tom and me. It's like we don't know how to express ourselves directly anymore. She has to put the words in our mouths for us and then coach us to repeat after her. "Tell him that you want this to work," she encourages me. "Tell her what you just said to me about missing her," she says to Tom.

Christmas Day, once festivities are done, I invite Tom to go for a drive with me. We have mostly been avoiding each other. Any time we spend together alone is rare and strained, but he agrees to go anyway. We make small talk about work and the kids. As we pull back up to the house, I pause before turning off the engine.

"You know this is hard for me, too, right?" I ask.

"I don't know anything about you anymore," comes his dejected reply.

I stare at his left hand resting on the console between us. I have always loved Tom's hands. They are big, strong, tough hands that have always made me feel safe and loved. A stirring deep in my gut kind of a little bit wants to hold that hand. I pause for a few beats and decide to go for it. The moment of contact startles him, and he draws away.

"Can I hold your hand for a minute?" I quickly plead.

"Sure," he concedes with a shrug. He relaxes and intertwines his fingers in mine. He stares out the front windshield. I look at his face for what feels like the first time in years. I see the deepened stress lines on his forehead and around his eyes. Have I made this whole thing up? Is it too big to overcome? I stare at his lips for a long moment.

"Can I kiss you?" I whisper. We make out in the front seat of my car like awkward teenagers for a few minutes. Once we get inside the house, I lead him to my bedroom…our bedroom. I lie back on the bed as I have so many times over our past fifteen years together. It feels at once so familiar, yet somehow foreign.

He crawls up beside me and pauses long enough for me to glance down, checking if he's okay. His eyes search mine for a long moment before he asks, "Can I touch you?"

"Yes," I respond with renewed faith. "I want you to."

****

If you've ever been too scared to go for what you really want because you might upset those you love, I challenge you to take a first step toward personal revelation by downloading the Study Guide for Chapter 11, which can be found at theuntherapist.com/chapter11. This guide will help you figure out how to help yourself, how to know when it's time to get outside help, and also how to know if the practitioner you choose is the right match for your specific needs.

Chapter 12

The Untherapy Way

Chapter Framework:

-Old belief (before Untherapy): I must be careful. It is not safe to expose who I really am to others. Vulnerability is dangerous. When people find out who I really am, they will reject me, and it will hurt even more than if I had protected myself. I am never good enough to fully trust that I'll be able to survive whatever comes my way.

-The Untherapy Perspective: We are co-creators of our reality, together with one another and the Divine. We get to decide how much we enjoy our lives. Life is naturally self-correcting. We can afford to take big risks because the Divine is even bigger and is always rigging the odds in our favor. Intentionally practicing public vulnerability creates the safest environment in which to grow and evolve. Becoming woundable actually creates the best chance to live a fully embodied life that expresses our true purpose and passion. Every experience is redeemable. Life is about learning. Every misstep or failure has inherent lessons that are useful for our continued advancement. We cannot help but succeed.

Quote: "Life is fun, nothing is sacred, and God is always changing" –Luke Jasinski

Within a matter of days, the awakening (as I have named the events of the past three months) has begun to solidify within me. Slowly, carefully, Tom and I navigate the landmine of harsh words, hurt feelings, and misunderstandings that litter every inch of the path we tread. Tom moves back into our bedroom. We once again spend our nights wrapped in each other's arms.

As the passage of days puts distance between the pain of those months of separation and the reconstruction of the present, I notice how different Tom is. All the frustrations I had before seem to be resolved. I feel good about helping Tom with the painting business, and he works hard to make time for me to work on Untherapy. When something bothers me, I don't hesitate to talk about it. I seem incapable of avoiding hard conversations, and the thought of stuffing my emotions down makes me want to throw up. When we get stuck, we stop what we are doing and work it out. We have our first yelling fight.

Tom mistakes my smirk for dismissive hubris. I scream back at the top of my lungs, "I'm not laughing at you. I'm making this face because I'm scared!"

He kicks the kitchen cabinet as hard as he can and yells back, "I'm scared too! I love you and I hate this, but I don't know how to talk to you right now!"

We both learn to say, "I need you to stop talking and really listen to me" and also "I am really trying to listen to you right now." After we are calmed down, we talk about what we learned and correct each other's misunderstandings. Oftentimes, it feels like we are two little kids just discovering how to use our words. And just like little kids, we end these conversations by hugging it out. I am able to let Tom be his own person who sometimes makes no sense to me at all. And I still want to be around him. Even when I am triggered, I find that I am able to access a place of Divine connection that allows me the time and space to decide how to respond. My higher self can hover above my struggling humanity and advise or support without getting lost in the scuffle.

In January of 2020, we celebrate our fifteen-year anniversary back in the Dominican Republic, being careful to avoid swimming in the ocean under red flag conditions. We treat it like an overdue honeymoon, spending the majority of our time testing out the mattress in our luxury suite.

Upon returning home, I develop a sudden onset of severe gastric distress. I have trouble eating and learn to stay in close proximity to a bathroom at all times. As I exhaust all the standard homeopathic and medical remedies to no avail, I begin searching for possible emotional causes. The common wisdom is that this bodily response indicates poor self-image and an inability to nourish my own soul (waiting for others to do it for me). Ten days into this misery, with no relief in sight, I come across an article discussing the fourth trauma response. In addition to the commonly known fight, flight, and freeze responses, there is another: fawning. Fawning is defined by the following behaviors:

- People-pleasing
- Being unable to say how you really think or feel
- Caring for others to your own detriment
- Always saying "yes" to requests
- Flattering others
- Struggling with low self-esteem
- Avoiding conflict
- Feeling taken advantage of
- Being very concerned about fitting in with others

I have labeled myself an Obliger ever since I first discovered Gretchen Rubin's Four Tendencies, and I have worked hard to organize my thoughts according to the five-star review I always seem to seek (especially from Tom, my kids, and close friends). What if all that was just a trauma response? What if, instead of freezing, fleeing, or fighting, I just people-please my way out of trauma triggers? I read the list of behaviors again. That old familiar sensation of falling knocks the wind out of me once again. Have I really been teaching this model for years, helping countless others discover and explain their own behavior and that of their loved ones without accurately identifying my own?

I compare myself to other Obligers I know. I can clearly see a level of self-satisfaction in the way they serve others that does not come naturally for me. I don't actually feel drawn to serving and helping unless I'm freaking out and melting down. If I'm not an Obliger, then what am I? I consider what I would do if I weren't triggered. How do I naturally respond when trauma is not informing my responses? I try each of the other thought models on for size. I'm definitely not a Rebel. I know so many Rebels, and their thought clouds defy my most open-minded understanding. The Questioner model doesn't fit, either. I'm naturally decisive and confident, and the puzzle-solving format feels overwhelming. Then it hits me. Oh my god—I'm an Upholder! The myriad of internal constructs that keep me in line are my thought boxes! I don't need to fight against them or try to subvert their power in favor of external rules. I get to make my own rules, based on my best understanding of how my world works!

I wake up the next morning with not a trace of the gastrointestinal distress that has ruled my life for the past ten days. I take this as a clear sign that my body has effectively communicated: message received!

For the first several weeks after this revelation, I am riddled with resistance against this newfound truth. I remember Gretchen Rubin's explanation about how Upholders tend to tighten around their rules. If I had a penny for every time Tom said the phrase, "There you go, making another rule!" I realize that my resistance to being who I truly am has everything to do with my old programming about how women are supposed to help, serve, and nurture (aka be Obligers). Accepting what I really am over the idea of what I should be requires a major shift in consciousness.

By now, I have come to trust Divine timing, believing that things come up at just the right time because they are ready to come out. Moving forward, I am now able to notice whenever I feel compelled to oblige a person or situation that it is actually the fawning trauma response. I can ask myself what is coming up so I can release it rather than defend it.

Armed with this new insight, I go back and reevaluate the breakdown I experienced with Tom. In those three months of misery, it was as if the final vestiges of my old, broken self all gathered forces in one giant attack on my self-concept. As an Upholder, I now understand why I fought so hard to maintain the rules and regulations that helped me survive my childhood and first marriage. For thirty years, one way of doing things worked: do what you're told, follow their rules, and trust that you'll be taken care of. Ever since Tom and I got together, I have been on a steady march toward healing, freedom, and a way of life where I consent to and take responsibility for everything that happens to me. I do not owe anything to anyone, and I suddenly find a seemingly infinite ability to extend unconditional love to others.

I enjoy embracing my newfound continuity. Boundaries are suddenly easy to enforce. I naturally become a master at identifying people and situations that are a match for me. For instance, right around this time, a close friend experiences a major life crisis and lashes out at me in the process. I am able to recognize that we are no longer a match and grieve the loss without the typical codependent yearnings for restoration.

I become acutely aware of the voice in my head, my own personal Creative Genius that is controlled and manipulated by me alone. I recognize how I have used my voice as a fear tactic to keep myself in line, even applying the sound of Tom's voice to add authority. For instance, whenever Tom would walk into a room where I was sitting and relaxing, I would imagine him angrily snapping, "Why aren't you doing something productive?" I realize he has never once actually said these words or acted this way, but my Creative Genius, supported by years of Supportive Supercomputer programming, has kept this ongoing dialogue close at hand to make sure I never relaxed or forgot my place.

The profound realization that I get to pick the story I tell in my own head is a total game changer. When I'm afraid, I admit it. When I'm triggered, I own it and work on releasing whatever came up so it can heal. When I'm scared, I give myself a reality check. When I'm confused, I ask for clarification. If Tom (or anyone, for that matter) does something I don't like or don't understand, I use my words to get more information before I decide what is actually happening.

I practice tuning in to the feeling of internal expansion that occurs when I trust the still small voice inside that prompts me to move toward one thing and away from another. I learn that this voice never forces, controls, or bullies me. It always comforts, encourages, protects, and challenges me. Listening to these inner promptings takes a new, deeper level of patience, trust, and vulnerability. Whenever I follow this guidance, I feel emotionally exposed, like a child who forgot to put her pants on before showing up to class. But the rewards are addicting. I feel fully alive and in possession of my personhood. This is my jam!

To develop this emotional muscle, I start what I call a public vulnerability practice. I set a daily intention to do at least one thing that exposes my soft underside to someone outside of me. Some days, this means having a hard conversation with Tom about something that scares me. For instance, when I trigger, I tend to become verbally aggressive. After I've been sharp, I go back and apologize, talking it out to figure out a better approach for next time. Other times, my public vulnerability practice looks like a Facebook Live video on my Untherapist page, where I share something that makes me nervous to talk about. I lean into discomfort whenever it calls me deeper into self-discovery. I don't always get it right, but I always learn something compelling, and I never regret the effort. The braver I act, the more courageous I become.

Feeling happy, relaxed, and optimistic becomes my normal setting. When I am gripped with fear, anxiety, or depression, I learn to notice what is coming up and even look forward to the process of releasing it to make space for more healing. My capacity to inhabit the present moment expands exponentially. For the first time in our marriage, I start looking for excuses to be carefree and silly with Tom, just because it feels good and I can. Our compatibility is undeniable, and our love at long last feels effortless. As the year 2020 progresses, rife with pandemic fears, racial tensions, and political upheaval, we experience an ever-deepening connection that draws us closer together. Is he still the one? The question no longer scares me.

Yes, Tom is the perfect match for me. The irony is, I wasn't able to really know this in my bones until I uncovered a far greater truth. "Is he still the one?" is actually the wrong question. My quest to answer it drew me into a deeper awareness of my own power and selfhood. The real question is: am I brave enough to choose to be my own "one"? Will I continue, step by step, to choose those paths, relationships, and challenges that transform me into the fullness of who I really am? Am I going to choose to be brave enough to lean into the not-knowing? Can I exist in the space between who I thought I was supposed to be and who I am capable of becoming? Will I trust that the uncertainty inherent in vulnerability is the only safe place to find truth?

Yes. The answer is yes.

****

If you love the ideas this chapter presents about living a life that creates amazing opportunities for happiness and fulfillment on purpose, I would like to invite you to join the Untherapy Academy. We are a unique, distraction-free community that is focused on simplifying our relationships so we can enjoy life. The group includes:

a) Ongoing weekly live support and coaching
b) Access to an ever-expanding library of essential on-demand courses
c) Membership in a community of like-minded people
d) Additional bonuses and resources to support your journey to simplify and improve all your most important relationships, especially the one with yourself

Find out more at theuntherapist.com/UntherapyAcademy.

Appendix

The Untherapy Model of Human Behavior

This model is a simple way to understand yourself and others that naturally optimizes connection and empathy. It is designed to be self-administered, thereby reconnecting you with your innate ability to heal yourself. Untherapy reawakens you to your inner knowing. Untherapy is not anti-therapy. The goal is to become more self-aware and emotionally literate so that when you do need outside help, you have the ability to choose the modality and practitioner that best suit your specific needs. It also enables you to apply the help in the best way possible to expedite your healing process.

Untherapy consists of three parts. For a downloadable diagram that illustrates the following description, go to theuntherapist.com/model.

Part One: The Head

The Head centers around your conscious mind, which is referred to as your Creative Genius. This is the part of the system where all your power lies. Your thoughts determine your choices, which influence your entire life. You have one of four thought models, adapted from Gretchen Rubin's Four Tendencies. Each person has only one thought model, and it remains the same for your entire life. Your thought model is optimized for your particular needs and works best for your unique life purpose and passions.

Rebels' thoughts are organized like clouds, which is to say, they are not actually organized. Rebels prefer to have wide open, flexible options. If someone tries to remove a cloud from a Rebel's field of potentiality, that is going to be the exact cloud they decide they most need. Rebels like to try different thoughts, sometimes releasing something that is already working just to make space for a change. They are famous for thinking outside the box and maintaining a naturally carefree spirit well into adulthood.

Upholders organize their thoughts like boxes. They love the rigid structure afforded by lots of rules, regulations, and defined parameters. These are all applied in the highly individualized manner that each Upholder personally prefers, so it's not that all rules are created equal. They pick and choose those that work for them based on what organizes their boxes best. Upholders tend to fixate on how things should be done and often tighten around rigid ways of thinking when they feel their rules are being challenged.

Questioners organize their thoughts like puzzles. Each thought is like a separate puzzle piece, and they are forever researching and collecting more information so they can make the right pieces fit together. Questioners can easily become bogged down in analysis paralysis, as it is difficult to decide exactly when enough data has been gathered.

Obligers organize their thoughts to accomplish a five-star review. Their thoughts are optimized to consider the effect they will have on the people and circumstances they are involved with. Obligers experience the most fulfillment and satisfaction when they can produce a result that meets or exceeds the expectations of all parties and creates a positive feedback loop. It is easy for Obligers to get bogged down in people-pleasing and forget to oblige themselves. But their desire to serve is distinct from the fawning response to trauma, which can manifest in any of the thought models to neutralize a trigger. In my work with clients, I have discovered that many people misdiagnose themselves as Obligers simply because they consider their trauma response when picking a thought model. Obligers always find deep fulfillment in serving and meeting expectations, independent of a triggered state.

Part Two: The Heart

The Heart is the seat of your feelings. Just as with your thought model, you also have a feeling type. This is called your Force of Nature, and you have only one of the following: Wind, Fire, Ocean, or Mountain. Your feeling type is optimized for your particular needs and works best for your unique life purpose and passions. The easiest way to feel better is to align more fully with your Force of Nature.

Winds naturally want to feel light and flexible. They need lots of options and the ability to disconnect from the thick of the ground level drama to float above with a bird's-eye view of life.

Fires naturally want to feel grounded while also being fueled with the energy of consuming and producing. They love to accomplish things and often do lots of projects just for fun. They are good at completing and naturally have the 80 percent rule figured out.

Oceans have an energy that goes from surface level down to the depths of emotion and intensity. To feel good, Oceans need lots of time and space to process in a methodical and cyclical manner (think waves, currents, and tides). Oceans love to hang out in the deep, where the pressure of rare thoughts and feelings brings them comfort and solace.

Mountains need stability, structural integrity, and lots of quiet time. To feel good, they must achieve internal homeostasis. They are great at self-reflection and prefer to say less while thinking more.

Unlike your thoughts, your feelings exist beyond conscious choice. They are housed in the subconscious mind, referred to in Untherapy as your Supportive Supercomputer. It is called a "supercomputer'' because it is an infinitely complex server farm of neurons that constantly work to provide the most beneficial information to support your every conscious thought. It is called "supportive" because it is designed to support your ultimate growth, healing, and evolution as it assists you in pursuing your desires. Your Supportive

Supercomputer does not have a separate personality or capacity to form opinions or make decisions on its own. Scientists estimate the subconscious mind can process twenty million bits of information per second, contrasted with only forty bits of info per second for the conscious mind (our Creative Genius). This means your Supportive Supercomputer processes five hundred thousand times faster than your Creative Genius.

This explains how, for example, you blink to protect your eye from a spatter of bacon grease before you are even consciously aware that your eyeball was in danger. This also explains what occurs behind the scenes when your Creative Genius decides to go after a big goal. Without forming an opinion either way, your Supportive Supercomputer faithfully pulls up all the necessary reference information (programs) in its extensive files, including your current knowledge and experience pertaining to that topic, awareness of what you still need to discover, and all related memories and associated traumas that have ever happened in the past.

Untherapy uses the metaphor of apps on a smartphone to illustrate the way these programs work. The most powerful of these apps were installed and populated with information before you were old enough to start kindergarten. Using this model, it is easier to understand why your Creative Genius can really, *really* want something, while your Supportive Supercomputer simultaneously floods you with debilitating fear, reinforced by every memory, trauma, and reference point that make you feel like you could never have it.

For instance, as I healed from the abuse of my first marriage, my Creative Genius started wanting to make my own choices and exercise my own power. Every time I dug into deeper levels of vulnerability and freedom, my Supportive Supercomputer would replay a vast array of apps from childhood (good girls are quiet and compliant) all the way through my first marriage (please God by submitting to your husband). Even though Tom had a perfect record of supporting my healing and wanted nothing more than for me to make my own decisions, a data dump from my Supportive Supercomputer would trigger anxiety attacks, depressive episodes, and Tom's angry voice in my head justifying all my deepest fears. To be clear, this was a voice that only existed in my fearful mind and had replaced the previous voices of my dad during childhood and Brad during my first marriage.

Untherapy teaches several methods of release, including a simple, gentle, tapping-based protocol called Superlearning that allows you to let go of these negative programs, along with all their associated emotions. Now that area of your life heals naturally.

Part 3: Core

Your Core houses your innermost desires. These are defined as internal perceptions of wanting something. Your desires are constantly inspired by your connection to the Divine. Untherapy teaches that "desire is proof of deserve," meaning that the very fact that you experience a longing or preference for something means you are capable of receiving the gift it brings. This does not mean that each desire is in its final form. Desires can only be interpreted through your thoughts about your feelings, which are in a constant state of healing from trauma and unsupportive programming. However, if you acknowledge a desire and take a step toward realizing its presence in your life, the journey will self-correct. Opposition, fear, and restrictive programming will come up to be released. As healing progresses, you will be able to understand more clearly how that desire is guiding you into a deeper expression of your fullest self.

Typically, this process takes you from initial levels of specific desire to broader, more inclusive goals. For example, in Chapter 11, I acknowledged my desire to begin my career as the Untherapist full time. Initially, I attached that goal to a specific timeframe. As I took imperfect steps toward that end, many fears and traumas presented for healing. As I worked through them, I became aware of a deeper desire that was much less committed to when this dream would happen and much more committed to *whom* it would be accomplished with.

The Untherapy system is built on the idea that as you pursue your deepest core desires, your Supportive Supercomputer is faithful to bring up the exact traumas and unsupportive programs in the right form and at the perfect time so they can be released and transformed. This makes space and creates momentum so you can progress toward your goals and dreams with grace and ease. Untherapy does not focus on limiting beliefs per se, because the above process does not require them to be searched out and discovered as an independent exercise. As you pursue your desires, limiting beliefs will naturally come up when they are ready to come out. This is always at just the right time and with the appropriate motivation to perpetuate forward motion.

People often ask if there is an online assessment to discover your thought model and feeling type. Untherapy is a self-diagnosing system. Because of the complex interplay between programming, trauma, and your natural thoughts and feelings, the most accurate way to discover the truth of who you are is to figure it out for yourself. Sometimes there is a process of trial and error in determining your thought model, feeling type, or in my case, both!

If you would like assistance in this process, I invite you to join the Untherapy Academy, where we will work together to figure out exactly which thought model and feeling type are accurate for you (as well as the other important people in your life). Find out more information about joining the Untherapy Academy at theuntherapist.com/UntherapyAcademy.

The Untherapy Perspective

Untherapy is a perpetually evolving set of beliefs that center around the importance of courage, simplicity, and consent in all relationships. Here are some of the main ideas. For the most up-to-date list, visit theuntherapist.com/beliefs.

-I am the main character in my own life, which means I am responsible for everything about me. I remember that this is true for every human.

-My unique combination of thought model, feeling type, life experiences, and true desires are perfectly optimized to support my best life.

-Existence is evidence of worthiness. By nature of the fact that I am alive in this time and space, I accept that who I truly am (thoughts, feelings, and desires) is who I was meant to be, and that's a good thing.

-I recognize the supportive nature of life and believe that powers larger than my comprehension are working behind the scenes to support my growth and healing.

-I am wired for connection, so it is important to get good at it. The more I understand about myself and others, the easier and more fulfilling all my relationships become.

-Things come up to come out. When something bothers me, I acknowledge that it has presented itself to be released. As I process these triggers, I make space for healing and growth in a natural, gentle process that works with and expands my capacity to thrive. By the same token, traumatic experiences provide the precise healing opportunities I am most ready for.

-"Desire is proof of deserve." When I want something, I recognize that this desire is directly connected to the best next steps for me. I notice my desires and pursue them with intention and consistency. I release my attachment to specific outcomes, knowing that course corrections will continue to perfect my path.

-Every experience is redeemable. Life is about learning. I acknowledge that every misstep or failure has inherent lessons that are useful (and maybe even essential) for my continued evolution.

-Everyone is doing their best with what they have from where they are. Even (and especially) when I cannot understand why, I recognize that each person got to this moment the same way I did: by trying to figure it out the best way they knew how.

-Life is meant to be enjoyed. I release the need to force and control my outcomes. I trust that as I consent to the choices I most desire, I will receive what is best for me.

-Negative feelings like fear, doubt, and anger are just as useful as positive ones. They draw attention to things I might otherwise ignore. As I process and release these emotions, I create space for my own evolution while simultaneously giving others permission to do the same.

-I take responsibility for communicating. I do not hold others responsible for things I have not clearly communicated. I do not expect others to read my mind.

-Life is a non-zero-sum game. Everyone can win. My having more does not equal less for you. Lack is an illusion that challenges me to process my negative emotions and further my understanding.

-Processing emotions does not have to be torturous. Because I am wired for healing and growth, releasing negative emotions can be gentle and natural. When I use the proper protocols, my personal evolution becomes a normal experience that gives meaning and purpose to my existence.

-Untherapy is a living belief system that is perpetually evolving as my consciousness expands.

For the latest updates, please visit theuntherapist.com. To participate in the evolution, join the Untherapy Academy at theuntherapist.com/UntherapyAcademy.

About the Author

Anne-Lise Jasinski is an emotional literacy educator and creator of The Untherapy Model of Human Behavior. She has over a decade of experience coaching and teaching in a variety of settings. Anne-Lise started out in corporate training and moved on to teaching in the university setting. As her system evolved, she shifted her focus toward individuals and small groups. Besides weekend group workshops and marriage and family counseling, she conducted hundreds of one-on-one sessions, both in person and online. When the pandemic hit, she transitioned her focus to online education, creating the Untherapy Academy. This community is the realization of her ultimate goal: to provide the kind of supportive environment that would have best helped her through her own struggles.

Today, the Untherapy Academy is the go-to resource for anyone who is ready to crack the code on their life and relationships. Members have access to an ever-expanding library of on-demand courses that reveal the secrets to creating the life they've always wanted. Anne-Lise hangs out in the community to teach, coach, and encourage members as they learn about themselves and the people who most affect them. Her greatest joy is to share with others the clarity and understanding that has turned her life around.

When Anne-Lise is not busy with the Academy or writing her next book, she enjoys spending time with her husband, Tom, their two pit bulls, Penny and Blue, and their kids (when they visit) but mostly Ella, since she still lives at home. She enjoys dancing, yoga, a moderate number of hardy houseplants, kombucha, meeting new people, and audiobooks.

Acknowledgements

A word on the order in which your name appears: other than Tom and immediate family, you are listed in chronological order from when you first appeared in my life.

Thank you first and foremost to my favorite Wind Rebel, Tom. Writing this book has reminded me all over again of what an amazing match we are. Thank you, thank you, thank you for choosing me. This adventure is starting to get exciting!

Thank you, Mom, my dear Wind Obliger, for birthing me, raising me, loving me, and always feeding me lots of good food. You are so much stronger than I ever realized. It wasn't until I wrote this book that I began to grasp the depth of impact you've had on my becoming who I am today. I love you so much more than would make you comfortable.

Thank you, Dad, the model of a Mountain Upholder if there ever was one, for believing in my talents and being proud of my achievements. Thank you for investing in this project. Your support has been everything in perfect timing. I hope you like it.

Thank you to all my siblings for being my original social group. We shared a pretty remarkable childhood, and I love that we have all managed to find our way back to each other as adults. Neil, my dear Mountain Obliger big brother, thank you for always treating me like I've got it going on. Stephanie, my beautiful Wind Rebel, thank you for being my original best friend and a treasured connection to this day. Jonathan, my crazy Wind Obliger brother, thank you for trusting me with your challenges and your art. Abigail, thank you for showing us the Mountain grace of well-planned intention and for Upholding right there with me. Ruth, my Ocean Obliger baby sister, thank you for treating me like a special mentor. I love when you call me!

Thank you, Gideon, my Ocean Questioner firstborn, for making me a mother and for teaching me more about unconditional love than I ever knew was possible. It is so rewarding to watch you thrive and succeed at life. I will never stop learning from our connection. You and Courtney make adulting look good!

Thank you, Hannah, my Wind Rebel sweetheart, for being the delightful daughter I knew you would be. Thank you for still baby-talking with me (we are hilarious). I know you are going to make an amazing mother, because you already are, and you don't even have any kids yet! You and Tyler are going to make beautiful babies.

Thank you, Luke, my Mountain Upholder son, for your patience and longsuffering. I know you picked me as your mom for a reason. I adore your creative spirit and esoteric musings. Please remember that I am cheering you on from here as you find your ambition. It's fun to watch you and Kayla go out into the world as modern hippies on this grand adventure we call life!

Thank you, Ella, my Wind Questioner firecracker, for setting the example of living life to the fullest. You are an athlete in every sense of the word, approaching life with a gusto and determination that is unrivaled. And thank you for your advanced emotional intelligence and communication skills. It's a pretty unique and powerful gift that will serve you in all aspects of your life. And I'm especially enjoying having instant access to it while you still live at home. Go make that money, my favorite rock star!

Thank you to Penny, my beautiful blonde pit bull (and Mountain Questioner—if dogs had a people personality), for holding vigil on the massage table during my early morning writing sessions. I loved you from the moment I met you, and no one can convince me you're not part human. Thank you for the deep conversations we have with our eyes.

Thank you, Brené Brown, for deciding to start a global conversation around shame and worthiness...and then doing it. Your work formed the foundation of my entire Untherapy shame resilience protocol. You are an amazing human with superhuman prowess. Your courage has blessed my life in all the best ways. At the risk of overstepping, I'm going to guess your thought model is Upholder, and I think your feeling type is either Ocean or Mountain. If you're curious, say the word, and we'll figure it out!

Thank you, Amber Robertson, my dear Mountain Rebel friend, for believing in my work before I did, for always pushing me upward and onward, and for cheering for me whenever I do hard things. Thank you for being the bridge between Tom and me when we needed it most. You were the only person who knew both of us well enough to hold space and help guide us back to each other. Also, thank you for being so willing to lend your photographic genius to my every whim. Your ability to capture the raw emotion and vulnerability of a moment on camera is second to none. I think I will always be "chasing Amber". Let's do it again soon.

Thank you, Travis Reed, for coming up after the Joplin tornado and making a film that beautifully expressed the pain, hope, destruction, and redemption in the aftermath of that disaster. Your artistic eye, Wind Rebel spirit, and insane goofiness were the perfect salve for our wounded souls. Your creative talent for conveying the hope, strength, beauty, and messiness of humanity is a world apart. *The Work of the People* is a gift to humanity. Let's make more art together sometime soon!

Thank you, Rob Bell, for giving historical context to the Bible, humanizing its authors, and helping me see its message of hope and redemption. Your work restored my faith, healed my religious wounds, and allowed me to recognize the literary and spiritual value of the best-selling book of all time. If I had to guess (which I always do), I would place you as a Mountain Rebel, but I would love to have a conversation and find out for sure!

Thank you, Gretchen Rubin, for developing the Four Tendencies framework and being an amazing Upholder. You provided the missing piece in my personality puzzle that brought this whole behavior model to life. I'm pretty sure your feeling type is Ocean, but I try not to assume. Would love to figure it out together if you're curious!

Thank you, Elizabeth Gilbert, for teaching me that "tortured artist" doesn't have to be a thing, and for writing *City of Girls*—one of the most awesome stories I've ever read. I love Vivian Morris! You're most likely a Rebel, and I'd love to figure out your feeling type!

Thank you, Glennon Doyle, for being the inspiration and example of how to write a book with fierce vulnerability. Every book you write is more compelling than the last. *Untamed* was a masterpiece I couldn't put down. Thank you for sharing your gift with the world. Someday I would love to meet you and figure out if my guess of Mountain Rebel is accurate for you.

Thank you, Mike Dooley, for making it your life's work to ask the big questions. More importantly, thank you for being open to hear the mind-blowing answers the Universe gave back. And for putting into words my deepest-held beliefs. Finding your work was like coming home to the most beautiful place I never knew existed. You are the one I listen to when I'm reeling from life's curveballs. I listen to you a lot. Also, in case you're curious, my guess is you are a Wind Questioner. I love being part of your community.

Thank you, Kayla Hollis, for your bright, sunshiny, Wind Obliger demeanor and your impressive artistic talent. Thank you for being able to take ideas straight out of my head and create sketches that fit perfectly. Whatever you do in life, please keep making art. Our world needs that. And thank you for falling in love with Luke. You two are perfect for each other!

Thank you, Julie Barkley, my sweet Wind Rebel book sensei, for being brave and always giving me wonderful feedback, even when you were worried it was too critical. Thank you for being available at all hours of the day and night to read a revision, ask an important question, and give the best cheerleading at the precise moments when my doubt had knocked me down. And thank you for the energy healing sessions. You have an amazing gift, and I'm honored to grow with you as you share your healing talent with the world. You will bless so many others. You are a treasured friend.

Thank you, Maddie Poppe, for being an amazing singer and songwriter. Special thanks for writing "Not Losing You". Every time I listen to it, I still get goosebumps and feel that transcendent awareness that you wrote it for me. Look for me at your next live concert!

Thank you, Gin Stephens, for the "Intermittent Fasting Stories" podcast. The first episode I listened to was Episode 86, which was your interview with Paul Brodie, and within that one hour, I went from someone who dreamed of maybe one day writing a book to scheduling the initial phone interview with Paul. Thank you also for introducing me to the OMAD IF lifestyle. Writing in the fasted state gave me clarity and productivity to spare. I think you are probably an Upholder as well. Upholders are often naturally good teachers, in my experience. It's probably all those boxes! And maybe an Ocean or Wind feeling type? I hope we can chat this one out!

Thank you, Paul Brodie, my book yoda, and the whole team at Brodie Publishing, for making the entire experience of writing my first book so effortless. The way you broke down the whole process into such simple, organized pieces tells me you must be an Upholder like me. Not sure on your feeling type, but I'd love to figure it out sometime!

Thank you, Ryan Levesque, for launching Bucket 2.0 at the precise moment in history that I most needed an awesome way to get this book out into the world. Your QuizFunnel Masterclass broke a complex process down into actionable steps that allowed me to implement the process while juggling a rigorous writing schedule and still slinging paint for sixty-plus hours a week. I would be very surprised if you weren't an Ocean Upholder.

Thank you, Rachel Rodgers and the whole Hello Seven team, for blowing the lid off my limiting mindset and showing me how to multiply my impact on the world. As always happens in my charmed life, you showed up at the precise moment when I was ready, and you have moved mountains for me just by being who you are. The "We Should All Be Millionaires" community has revolutionized my entire life. I'm pretty sure you're a Wind Rebel, and I just know I'm going to get a chance to confirm that in real life at some point in the future!

Thank you, Gina Bianchini and the entire team at Mighty Networks, for creating a platform on which the Untherapy Academy can thrive and grow as a dynamic community. You are, without question, my favorite software company in the universe. Your support, love, and passion for bringing people together is absolutely unrivaled. I am thrilled to be a member of your tribe!

Contact Information

Anne-Lise can be reached at
annelise@annelisetheuntherapist.com

Website:
https://theuntherapist.com/

Membership community:
https://theuntherapist.com/UntherapyAcademy

Facebook:
https://www.facebook.com/untherapyacademy

Feedback Request

Believe it or not, every review does matter. That includes you! If you loved this book, please consider leaving a review so others can find it more easily.

If you did *not* like this book, before you leave a bad review (unless that would just really make you feel better), please consider contacting me at annelise@annelisetheuntherapist.com to share how I can improve. I am always learning, so I will listen to you.

www.ingramcontent.com/pod-product-compliance
Lightning Source LLC
Chambersburg PA
CBHW072156090426
42740CB00012B/2284
9781734805338